D0053598

Back to Basics: Investing

by Eric Tyson, MBA

WILEY

Publisher's Acknowledgments

Editorial Project Manager:
Victoria M. Adang

Senior Acquisitions Editor:
Tracy Boggier

Production Editor: Antony Sami

Cover Images: (paper)
© tumdee / Getty Images, (arrow)
© LokFung / Getty Images

Cover Design: Wiley

Back to Basics: Investing

Published by John Wiley & Sons, Inc.
111 River St.
Hoboken, NJ 07030-5774
http://www.wiley.com

For general information on our other products and services, please contact our Business Development
Department in the U.S. at 317-572-3205.

ISBN 978-1-119-47250-6 (pbk); ISBN 978-1-119-47295-7 (ePub); ISBN 978-1-119-47294-0 (ePDF)

Manufactured in the United States of America

F10005509 102318

Contents

1

Your Investment Choices

In many parts of the world, life's basic necessities — food, clothing, shelter, and taxes — consume the entirety of people's meager earnings. Although some Americans do truly struggle for basic necessities, the bigger problem for other Americans is that they consider just about *everything* — eating out, driving new cars, hopping on airplanes for vacation — to be a necessity. However, I believe that investing — that is, putting your money to work for you — is a necessity. If you want to accomplish important personal and financial goals, such as owning a home, starting your own business, helping your kids through college, retiring comfortably, and so on, you must know how to invest well.

Simply stated, *investing* means you have money put away for future use.

You can choose from tens of thousands of stocks, bonds, mutual funds, exchange-traded funds, and other investments. Unfortunately for the novice, knowing the name of the investment is just the tip of the iceberg. Underneath each of these investments lurks a veritable mountain of details.

However, making wise investments need not take a lot of your time. If you know where to get high-quality information and you purchase well-managed investments, you can leave the investment management to the experts. Then you can do the work you're best at and have more free time for the things you really enjoy doing.

This chapter identifies the major investments and outlines the strengths and weaknesses of each.

Ownership Investments

If you want your money to grow faster than the rate of inflation over the long term and you don't mind a bit of a roller-coaster ride from time to time in your investments' values, ownership investments are for you. *Ownership investments* are those investments where you own an interest in some company or other asset (such as stock, real estate, or a small business) that has the ability to generate revenue and profits.

Observing how the world's richest have built their wealth is enlightening. Not surprisingly, many of the champions of wealth around the globe gained their fortunes largely through owning a piece (or all) of a successful company that they (or others) built.

In addition to owning their own businesses, many well-to-do people have built their nest eggs by investing in real estate and the stock market. With softening housing prices in many regions in the late 2000s, some folks newer to the real estate world incorrectly believe that real estate is a loser, not a long-term winner. Likewise, the stock market goes through down periods but does well over the long term.

If you understand and are comfortable with the risks and take sensible steps to *diversify* (you hold a variety of invest-ments), ownership investments are the key to building wealth. For most folks to accomplish typical longer-term financial goals, such as retiring, the money they save and invest needs to grow at a healthy clip. If you keep all your money in bank accounts that pay little if any interest, you're likely to fall short of your goals.

Not everyone needs to make his money grow, of course. Suppose you inherit a significant sum and/or maintain a restrained standard of living and work well into your old age simply because you enjoy doing so. In this situation, you may not need to take the risks involved with a potentially faster-growth investment. You may be more comfortable with *safer* investments, such as paying off your mortgage faster than necessary. Chapter 3 helps you think through such issues.

Stocks

Stocks, which are shares of ownership in a company, are an example of an ownership investment. If you want to share in the growth and profits of companies like Skechers (footwear), you can. You simply buy shares of their stock through a brokerage firm. However, even if Skechers makes money in the future, you can't guarantee that the value of its stock will increase.

Some companies today sell their stock directly to investors, allowing you to bypass brokers. You can also invest in stocks via a stock mutual fund (or an exchange-traded fund), where a fund manager decides which individual stocks to include in the fund.

_____

_____

_____

If you practice some simple lessons, such as making regular and systematic investments and investing in proven companies and funds while minimizing your investment expenses and taxes, you should make decent returns in the long term.

However, don't expect that you can "beat the markets," and you certainly can't beat the best professional money managers at their own full-time game. This book shows you time-proven, non-gimmicky methods to make your money grow in the stock market.

Real estate

People of varying economic means build wealth by investing in real estate. Owning and managing real estate is like running a small business. You need to satisfy customers (tenants), manage your costs, keep an eye on the competition, and so on. Some methods of real estate investing require more time than others, but many are proven ways to build wealth. If you're interested in this type of ownership investment, pick up my *Back to Basics: Real Estate Investing* book (Wiley).

Small business

Some people hit investing home runs by owning or buying businesses. Unlike the part-time nature of investing in the stock market, most people work full time at running their businesses, increasing their chances of doing something big financially with them.

If you try to invest in individual stocks, by contrast, you're likely to work at it part time, competing against professionals who invest practically around the clock. Even if you devote almost all your time to managing your stock portfolio, you're still a passive bystander in businesses run by others. When you invest in your own small business, you're the boss.

In addition to the potential for becoming a financially successful entrepreneur, many small-business owners enjoy the nonfinancial rewards, including the challenge and fulfillment of operating a successful business.

Lending Investments

Besides ownership investments, the other major types of investments include those in which you lend your money.

Suppose, like most people, you keep some money in your local bank — most likely in a checking account but perhaps also in a savings account or certificate of deposit (CD). No matter what type of bank account you place your money in, you're lending your money to the bank.

How long and under what conditions you lend money to your bank depends on the specific bank and the account that you use. With a CD, you commit to lend your money to the bank for a specific length of time — perhaps six months or even a year. In return, the bank probably pays you a higher rate of interest than if you put your money in a bank account offering you immediate access to the money. (You may demand termination of the CD early; however, you'll be penalized.)

As I discuss in Chapters 7 and 8, you can also invest your money in bonds, another type of lending investment. When you purchase a bond that's been issued by the government or a company, you agree to lend your money for a predetermined period of time and receive a particular rate of interest. A bond may pay you 4 percent interest over the next ten years, for example.

An investor's return from lending investments is typically limited to the original investment plus interest payments. If you lend your money to Skechers through one of its bonds that matures in, say, ten years, and Skechers triples in size over the next decade, you won't share in its growth. Skechers stockholders and employees reap the rewards of the company's success, but as a bondholder, you don't; you simply get interest and the face value of the bond back at maturity.

Many people keep too much of their money in lending investments, thus allowing others to reap the rewards of economic growth. Although lending investments appear safer because you know in advance what return you'll receive, they aren't that safe. The long-term risk of these seemingly safe money investments is that your money will grow too slowly to enable you to accomplish your personal financial goals.

2

Investment Risks
and Returns

Risk is in the eye of the beholder. Many people base their perception of risk, in large part, on their experiences and what they've been exposed to. In doing so, they often fret about relatively small risks while overlooking much larger risks.

In the world of investing, most folks worry about certain risks — some of which may make sense and some of which may not — but at the same time they completely overlook or disregard other, more significant risks. This chapter focuses on a range of investments and their risks and expected returns.

Evaluating Risks

Everywhere you turn, risks exist; some are just more apparent than others. Many people misunderstand risks. With increased knowledge, you may be able to reduce or conquer some of your fears and make more sensible decisions about reducing risks.

Although some people like to live life to its fullest and take "fun" risks (how else can you explain mountain climbers, parachutists, and bungee jumpers?), most people seek to minimize risk and maximize enjoyment in their lives. The vast majority of people also understand that they'd be a lot less happy living a life in which they sought to eliminate all risks, and they likely wouldn't be able to do so anyway.

Likewise, if you attempt to avoid all the risks involved in investing, you likely won't succeed, and you likely won't be happy with your investment results and lifestyle. In the investment world, some people don't go near stocks or any investment that they perceive to be volatile. As a result, such investors often end up with lousy long-term returns and expose themselves to some high risks that they overlooked, such as the risk of having inflation and taxes erode the purchasing power of their money.

You can minimize but never eliminate risks. Some methods of risk reduction aren't palatable because they reduce your quality of life. Risks are also composed of several factors. The sections that follow explain the various types of investment risks and reveal proven methods you can use to sensibly reduce these risks while not missing out on the upside that growth investments offer.

Market-value risk

Although the stock market can help you build wealth, most people recognize that it can also drop substantially — by 10, 20, or 30 percent (or more) in a relatively short period of time. After peaking in 2000, US stocks, as measured by the large-company S&P 500 index, dropped about 50 percent by 2002. Stocks on the NASDAQ, which is heavily weighted toward technology stocks, plunged more than 76 percent from 2000 through 2002!

After a multiyear rebound, stocks peaked in 2007 and then dropped sharply during the "financial crisis" of 2008. From peak to bottom, US and global stocks dropped by 50-plus percent.

In a mere six weeks (from mid-July 1998 to early September 1998), large-company US stocks fell about 20 percent. An index of smaller-company US stocks dropped 33 percent over a slightly longer period of two and a half months.

You may want to keep all your money in the bank — after all, you know you won't lose your money, and you won't have to be a nonstop worrier. But just letting your money sit around would be a mistake.

If you pass up the stock market simply because of the potential market value risk, you miss out on a historic, time-tested method of building substantial wealth. Instead of seeing declines and market corrections as horrible things, view them as potential opportunities or "sales." Try not to give in to the human emotions that often scare people away from buying something that others seem to be shunning.

Later in this chapter, I show you the generous returns that stocks have historically provided. The following sections suggest some simple things you can do to lower your investing risk and help prevent your portfolio from suffering a huge fall.

Diversify for stability

If you worry about the health of the US economy, the government, and the dollar, you can reduce your investment risk by investing overseas. Most large US companies do business overseas, so when you invest in larger US company stocks, you get some international investment exposure. You can also invest in international company stocks, ideally via mutual funds and exchange-traded funds (see Chapters 9 and 10).

Of course, investing overseas can't totally protect you in the event of a global economic catastrophe.

Consider your time horizon

Investors who worry that the stock market may take a dive and take their money down with it need to consider the length of time that they plan to invest. In a one-year period in the stock and bond markets, a wide range of outcomes can occur. History shows that you lose money about once in every three years that you invest in the stock and bond markets. However, stock market investors have made money approximately two-thirds of the time over a one-year period.

Although the stock market is more volatile than the bond market in the short term, stock market investors have earned far better long-term returns than bond investors have. (See the "Stock returns" section later in this chapter for details.) Why? Because stock investors bear risks that bond investors don't bear, and they can reasonably expect to be compensated for those risks. Remember, however, that bonds generally outperform bank accounts.

History has shown that the risk of a stock or bond market fall becomes less of a concern the longer that you plan to invest. Figure 2-1 shows that as the holding period for owning stocks increases from 1 year to 3 years to 5 years to 10 years and then to 20 years, there's a greater likelihood of seeing stocks increase in value. In fact, over any 20-year time span, the US stock market, as measured by the S&P 500 index of larger company stocks, has *never* lost money, even after you subtract the effects of inflation.

Most stock market investors are concerned about the risk of losing money. Figure 2-1 clearly shows that the key to minimizing the probability that you'll lose money in stocks is to hold them for the longer term. Don't invest in stocks unless you plan to hold them for at least five years — and preferably a decade or longer.

_____

_____

_____

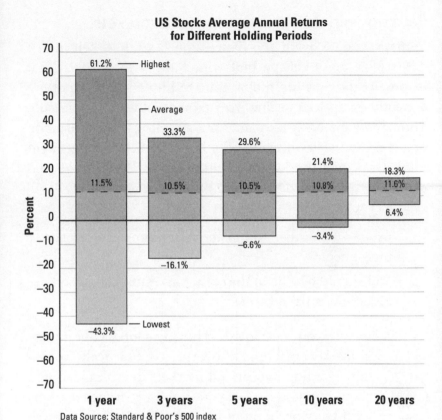

**US Stocks Average Annual Returns
for Different Holding Periods**

Data Source: Standard & Poor's 500 index

© John Wiley & Sons, Inc.

Figure 2-1: *The longer you hold stocks, the more likely you are to make money.*

Pare down holdings in overpriced markets

Perhaps you've heard the expression "buy low, sell high." Although I don't believe that you can *time the markets* (that is, predict the most profitable time to buy and sell), spotting a greatly overpriced or underpriced market isn't too difficult. Throughout this book, I explain some simple yet powerful methods you can use to measure whether a particular investment market is of fair value, of good value, or overpriced. You should avoid overpriced investments for two important reasons:

- If and when these overpriced investments fall, they usually fall farther and faster than more fairly priced investments.

- You should be able to find other investments that offer higher potential returns.

Ideally, you want to avoid having a lot of your money in markets that appear overpriced. Practically speaking, avoiding overpriced markets doesn't mean you should try to sell all of your holdings in such markets with the vain hope of buying them back at a much lower price. However, you may benefit from the following strategies:

- **Invest new money elsewhere.** Focus your investment of new money somewhere other than the overpriced market; put it into investments that offer you better values. As a result, without selling any of your seemingly expensive investments, you make them a smaller portion of your total holdings. If you hold investments outside of tax-sheltered retirement accounts, focusing your money elsewhere also allows you to avoid incurring taxes from selling appreciated investments.

- **If you have to sell, sell the expensive stuff.** If you need to raise money to live on, such as for retirement, or for a major purchase, sell the pricier holdings. As long as the taxes aren't too troublesome, it's better to sell high and lock in your profits.

Individual-investment risk

A downdraft can put an entire investment market on a roller-coaster ride, but healthy markets also have their share of individual losers. For example, from the early 1980s through the late 1990s, the US stock market had one of the greatest appreciating markets in history. You'd never know it, though, if you held one of the great losers of that period.

Consider a company now called Navistar, which has undergone enormous transformations in recent decades. This company used to be called International Harvester and manufactured farm equipment, trucks, and construction and other industrial equipment. Today, Navistar makes mostly trucks.

In late 1983, this company's stock traded at more than $140 per share. It then plunged more than 90 percent over the ensuing decade. Even with a rally in recent years, Navistar stock still trades at less than $20 per share (after dipping below $10 per share). Lest you think that's a big drop, this company's stock traded as high as $455 per share in the late 1970s! If a worker retired from this company in the late 1970s with $200,000 invested in the company stock, the retiree's investment would be worth about $6,000 today! On the other hand, if the retiree had simply swapped his stock at retirement for a diversified portfolio of stocks, his $200,000 nest egg would've instead grown to more than $5 million!

 Here are some simple steps you can take to lower the risk of individual investments that can upset your goals:

_____

_____

_____

- **Do your homework.** When you purchase stocks, you can examine some measures of value and the company's financial condition and business strategy to reduce your chances of buying into an overpriced company or one on the verge of major problems.

- **Diversify.** Investors who seek growth invest in securities such as stocks. Placing significant amounts of your capital in one or a handful of securities is risky, particularly if the stocks are in the same industry or closely related industries. To reduce this risk, purchase stocks in a variety of industries and companies within each industry.

- **Hire someone to invest for you.** The best funds (see Chapter 10) offer low-cost, professional management and oversight as well as diversification. Stock funds typically own 25 or more securities in a variety of companies in different industries.

Purchasing-power risk (aka inflation risk)

Increases in the cost of living (that is, inflation) can erode the value of your retirement resources and what you can buy with that money — also known as its *purchasing power*. When Teri retired at the age of 60, she was pleased with her retirement income. She was receiving an $800-per-month pension and $1,200 per month from money that she had invested in long-term bonds. Her monthly expenditures amounted to about $1,500.

Fast-forward 15 years. Teri still receives $800 per month from her pension, but now she gets only $900 per month of investment income, which comes from certificates of deposit. Teri bailed out of bonds after she lost sleep over the sometimes roller-coaster-like price movements in the bond market. Her monthly expenditures now amount to about $2,400, and she uses some of her investment principal (original investment). She's terrified of outliving her money.

Teri has reason to worry. She has 100 percent of her money invested without protection against increases in the cost of living. Although her income felt comfortable in the beginning of her retirement, it doesn't at age 75, and Teri may easily live another 15 or more years.

The erosion of the purchasing power of your investment dollar can, over longer time periods, be as bad as or worse than the effect of a major market crash. Table 2-1 shows the effective loss in purchasing power of your money at various rates of inflation and over differing time periods.

Inflation Rate	10 Years	15 Years	25 Years	40 Years
2%	–18%	–26%	–39%	–55%
4%	–32%	–44%	–62%	–81%
6%	–44%	–58%	–77%	–90%
8%	–54%	–68%	–85%	–95%
10%	–61%	–76%	–91%	–98%

Table 2-1: *Inflation's Corrosive Effect on Your Money's Purchasing Power*

Skittish investors often try to keep their money in bonds and money market accounts, thinking they are playing it safe. The risk in this strategy is that your money won't grow enough over the years for you to accomplish your financial goals. In other words, the lower the return you earn, the more you need to save to reach a particular financial goal.

A 40-year-old wanting to accumulate $500,000 by age 65 would need to save $722 per month if she earns a 6 percent average annual return, but she needs to save only $377 per month if she earns a 10 percent average return per year. Younger investors need to pay the most attention to the risk of generating low returns, but so should younger senior citizens. At the age of 65, seniors need to recognize that a portion of their assets may not be used for a decade or more from the present.

Analyzing Returns

When you make investments, you have the potential to make money in a variety of ways. Each type of investment has its own mix of associated risks that you take when you part with your investment dollar and, likewise, offers a different potential rate of return. In the following sections, I cover the returns you can expect with each of the common investing avenues. But first, I walk you through the components of calculating the total return on an investment.

The components of total return

To figure out exactly how much money you've made (or lost) on your investment, you need to calculate the *total return*. To come up with this figure, you need to determine how much money you originally invested and then factor in the other components, such as interest, dividends, and appreciation (or depreciation).

If you've ever had money in a bank account that pays *interest*, you know the bank pays you a small amount of interest when you allow it to keep your money. The bank then turns around and lends your money to some other person or organization at a much higher rate of interest. The rate of interest is also known as the *yield*. So if a bank tells you that its savings account pays 2 percent interest, the bank may also say that the account yields 2 percent. Banks usually quote interest rates or yields on an annual basis. Interest you receive is one component of the return you receive on your investment.

If a bank pays monthly interest, the bank also likely quotes a *compounded effective annual yield*. After the first month's interest is credited to your account, that interest starts earning interest as well. So the bank may say that the account pays 2 percent, which compounds to an effective annual yield of 2.04 percent.

When you lend your money directly to a company — which is what you do when you invest in a bond that a corporation issues — you also receive interest. Bonds, as well as stocks (which are shares of ownership in a company), fluctuate in value after they're issued.

When you invest in a company's stock, you hope that the stock increases *(appreciates)* in value. Of course, a stock can also decline, or *depreciate*, in value. This change in market value is part of your return from a stock or bond investment:

$$\frac{\text{Current investment value} - \text{Original investment}}{\text{Original investment}} = \text{Appreciation or depreciation}$$

For example, if one year ago you invested $10,000 in a stock (you bought 1,000 shares at $10 per share) and the investment is now worth $11,000 (each share is worth $11), your investment's appreciation looks like this:

$$\frac{\$11,000 - \$10,000}{\$10,000} = 10\%$$

Stocks can also pay *dividends*, which are the company's sharing of some of its profits with you as a stockholder. Some companies, particularly those that are small or growing rapidly, choose to reinvest all their profits back into the company. (Of course, some companies don't turn a profit, so they don't have anything to pay out!) You need to factor any dividends into your return as well.

Suppose that in the previous example, in addition to your stock appreciating from $10,000 to $11,000, it paid you a dividend of $100 ($1 per share). Here's how you calculate your total return:

$$\frac{(\text{Current investment value} - \text{Original investment}) + \text{Dividends}}{\text{Original investment}} = \text{Total return}$$

You can apply this formula to the example, like so:

$$\frac{(\$11,000-\$10,000)+\$100}{\$10,000}=11\%$$

Although you may be happy that your stock has given you an 11 percent return on your invested dollars, remember that unless you held your investment in a tax-sheltered retirement account, you owe taxes on your return. Specifically, the dividends and investment appreciation that you realize upon selling are taxed, although often at relatively low rates. The tax rates on so-called long-term capital gains and stock dividends are lower than the tax rates on other income.

If you've invested in savings accounts, money market accounts, or bonds, you owe federal income taxes on the interest.

Often, people make investing decisions without considering the tax consequences of their moves. This is a big mistake. What good is making money if the federal and state governments take away a substantial portion of it?

If you're in a moderate tax bracket, taxes on your investment probably run in the neighborhood of 30 percent (federal and state). So if your investment returned 6 percent before taxes, you're left with a return of about 4.2 percent after taxes.

Savings and money market account returns

You need to keep your extra cash that awaits investment (or an emergency) in a safe place, preferably one that doesn't get hammered by the sea of changes in the financial markets. By default and for convenience, many people keep their extra cash in a bank savings account. Although the bank offers the US government's backing via the Federal Deposit Insurance Corporation (FDIC), it comes at a price. Most banks pay a relatively low interest rate on their savings accounts. (I discuss banking options, including the sometimes higher-yielding online banks, in Chapter 7.)

Another place to keep your liquid savings is in a money market mutual fund. These are the safest types of mutual funds around and, for all intents and purposes, equal a bank savings account's safety. The best money market funds generally pay higher yields than most bank savings accounts. Unlike a bank, money market mutual funds tell you how much they deduct for the service of managing your money. See Chapter 7 for more on money market funds.

If you don't need immediate access to your money, consider using Treasury bills (T-bills) or bank certificates of deposit (CDs), which are usually issued for terms such as 3, 6, or 12 months. Your money will generally earn more in one of these vehicles than in a bank savings account. (In recent years, the yields on T-bills has been so low that the best FDIC-insured bank savings accounts have higher yields.) Rates vary by institution, so it's essential to shop around. The drawback to T-bills and bank certificates of deposit is that you incur a penalty (with CDs) or a transaction fee (with T-bills) if you withdraw your investment before the term expires (see Chapter 7).

Bond returns

When you buy a bond, you lend your money to the issuer of that bond (borrower), which is generally the federal government or a corporation, for a specific period of time. When you buy a bond, you expect to earn a higher yield than you can with a money market or savings account. You're taking more risk, after all. Companies can and do go bankrupt, in which case you may lose some or all of your investment.

Generally, you can expect to earn a higher yield when you buy bonds that

- **Are issued for a longer term:** The bond issuer is tying up your money at a fixed rate for a longer period of time.

- **Have lower credit quality:** The bond issuer may not be able to repay the principal.

Wharton School of Business professor Jeremy Siegel has tracked the performance of bonds and stocks back to 1802. Although the rate of inflation has increased since the early twentieth century, bond returns haven't increased over the decades. Long-term bonds maintained slightly higher returns in recent years than short-term bonds. The bottom line: Bond investors typically earn about 4 to 5 percent per year.

Stock returns

Investors expect a fair return on their investments. If one investment doesn't offer a seemingly high enough potential rate of return, investors can choose to move their money into other investments that they believe will perform better. Instead of buying a diversified basket of stocks and holding, some investors frequently buy and sell, hoping to cash in on the latest hot investment. This tactic seldom works in the long run.

Unfortunately, some of these investors use a rearview mirror when they purchase their stocks, chasing after investments that have recently performed strongly on the assumption (and the hope) that those investments will continue to earn good returns. But chasing after the strongest performing investments can be dangerous if you catch the stock at its peak, ready to begin a downward spiral. You may have heard that the goal of investing is to buy low and sell high. Chasing high-flying investments can lead you to buy high, with the prospect of having to sell low if the stock runs out of steam. Even though stocks as a whole have proved to be a good long-term investment, picking individual stocks is a risky endeavor. See Chapters 4 and 5 for my advice on making sound stock investment decisions.

A tremendous amount of data exists regarding stock market returns. In fact, in the US markets, data going back more than two centuries document the fact that stocks have been a terrific long-term investment. The long-term returns from stocks that investors have enjoyed, and continue to enjoy, have been remarkably constant from one generation to the next.

_____

_____

_____

Going all the way back to 1802, the US stock market has produced an annual return of 8.3 percent, while inflation has grown at 1.4 percent per year. Thus, after subtracting for inflation, stocks have appreciated about 6.9 percent faster annually than the rate of inflation. The US stock market returns have consistently and substantially beaten the rate of inflation over the years.

Stocks are the best long-term performers, but they have more volatility than bonds and Treasury bills. A balanced portfolio gets you most of the long-term returns of stocks without much of the volatility.

_____

_____

_____

3
Financial Strategies for Life

Before you make any wealth-building investments, I recommend that you get your financial house in order. Understanding and implementing some simple personal financial management concepts can pay off big for you in the decades ahead.

You probably want to know how to earn healthy returns on your investments without getting clobbered. Although you generally must accept greater risk to have the potential for earning higher returns (see Chapter 2), in this chapter, I tell you about some high-return, low-risk investments. My recommendations include some easy-to-tap opportunities for managing your money that you may have overlooked.

Emergency Reserves

You never know what life will bring, so having a readily accessible reserve of cash to meet unexpected expenses makes good financial sense.

 Make sure you have quick access to at least three months' to as much as six months' worth of living expenses. Keep this emergency money in a savings account or a money market fund (see Chapter 7).

If you don't have a financial safety net, you may be forced into selling an investment that you've worked hard for. And selling some investments, such as real estate, costs big money (because of transaction costs, taxes, and so on).

Debt

Yes, paying down debts is boring, but it makes your investment decisions less difficult. Rather than spending so much of your time investigating specific investments, paying off your debts (if you have them and your cash coming in exceeds the cash going out) may be your best high-return, low-risk investment. Consider the interest rate you pay and your investing alternatives to determine which debts you should pay off.

Consumer debt

Borrowing via credit cards, auto loans, and the like is an expensive way to borrow. Banks and other lenders charge higher interest rates for consumer debt than for debt for investments, such as real estate and business. The reason: Consumer loans are the riskiest type of loan for a lender.

Many folks have credit card or other consumer debt, such as an auto loan, that costs 8, 10, 12, or perhaps as much as 18-plus percent per year in interest. Reducing and eventually eliminating this debt with your savings is like putting your money in an investment with a guaranteed *tax-free* return equal to the rate that you pay on your debt.

For example, if you have outstanding credit card debt at 15 percent interest, paying off that debt is the same as putting your money to work in an investment with a guaranteed 15 percent tax-free annual return. Because the interest on consumer debt isn't tax deductible, you need to earn more than 15 percent by investing your money elsewhere in order to net 15 percent after paying taxes. Earning such high investing returns is highly unlikely, and in order to earn those returns, you'd be forced to take great risk.

Mortgage debt

Paying off your mortgage more quickly is an "investment" for your spare cash that may make sense for your financial situation. However, the wisdom of making this financial move isn't as clear as paying off high-interest consumer debt; mortgage interest rates are generally lower, and the interest is typically tax deductible.

When used properly, debt can help you accomplish your goals — such as buying a home or starting a business — and make you money in the long run. Borrowing to buy a home generally makes sense. Over the long term, homes generally appreciate in value.

If your financial situation has changed or improved since you first needed to borrow mortgage money, reconsider how much mortgage debt you need or want. Even if your income hasn't escalated or you haven't inherited vast wealth, your frugality may allow you to pay down some of your debt sooner than the lender requires.

When evaluating whether to pay down your mortgage faster, compare your mortgage interest rate with your investments' rates of return (defined in Chapter 2). Suppose you have a fixed-rate mortgage with an interest rate of 5 percent. If you decide to make investments instead of paying down your mortgage more quickly, your investments need to produce an average annual rate of return, before taxes, of about 5 percent to come out ahead financially.

Besides lacking the money to do so (the most common reason), other good reasons *not* to pay off your mortgage any quicker than necessary include the following:

- **You instead contribute to your retirement accounts, such as a 401(k), an IRA, or a SEP-IRA plan (especially if your employer offers matching money).** Paying off your mortgage faster has no tax benefit. By contrast, putting additional money into a retirement plan can immediately reduce your federal and state income tax burdens.

- **You're willing to invest in growth-oriented, volatile investments, such as stocks and real estate.** To have a reasonable chance of earning a greater return on your investments than it costs you to borrow on your mortgage, you must be aggressive with your investments. Stocks and real estate have produced annual average rates of return of about 8 to 9 percent.

- **Paying down the mortgage depletes your emergency reserves.** Psychologically, some people feel uncomfortable paying off debt more quickly if it diminishes their savings and investments. You probably don't want to pay down your debt if doing so depletes your financial safety cushion.

Don't be tripped up by the misconception that somehow a real estate market downturn will harm you more if you pay down your mortgage. Your home is worth what it's worth — its value has *nothing* to do with your debt load. Unless you're willing to walk away from your home and send the keys to the bank (also known as *default,* which damages your credit report and score), you suffer the full effect of a price decline, regardless of your mortgage size, if real estate prices drop.

_____

_____

_____

Financial Goals

You may have just one purpose for investing money, or you may desire to invest money for several different purposes simultaneously. Either way, you should establish your financial goals before you begin investing. Otherwise, you won't know how much to save.

Savings rate

To accomplish your financial goals (and some personal goals), you need to save money, and you also need to know your savings rate. Your *savings rate* is the percentage of your past year's income that you saved and didn't spend. Without even doing the calculations, you may already know that your rate of savings is low, nonexistent, or negative and that you need to save more.

Part of being a smart investor involves figuring out how much you need to save to reach your goals. Not knowing what you want to do a decade or more from now is perfectly normal — after all, your goals and needs evolve over the years. But that doesn't mean you should just throw your hands in the air and not make an effort to see where you stand today and think about where you want to be in the future.

An important benefit of knowing your savings rate is that you can better assess how much risk you need to take to accomplish your goals. Seeing the amount that you need to save to achieve your dreams may encourage you to take more risk with your investments.

During your working years, if you consistently save about 10 percent of your annual income, you're probably saving enough to meet your goals (unless you want to retire at a relatively young age). On average, most people need about 75 percent of their pre-retirement income throughout retirement to maintain their standard of living.

If you're one of the many people who don't save enough, you need to do some homework. To save more, you need to reduce your spending, increase your income, or both. For most people, reducing spending is the more feasible way to save.

To reduce your spending, first figure out where your money goes. You may have some general idea, but you need to have facts. Examine your checking account history, online bill-paying records, credit card bills, and any other documentation that shows your spending history. Tally up how much you spend on dining out, operating your car(s), paying your taxes, and everything else. After you have this information, you can begin to prioritize and make the necessary trade-offs to reduce your spending and increase your savings rate.

Investment preferences

Many good investing choices exist: You can invest in real estate, the stock market, mutual funds, exchange-traded funds, or your own or someone else's small business. Or you can pay down mortgage debt more quickly. What makes sense for you depends on your goals as well as your personal preferences. If you detest risk-taking and volatile investments, paying down your mortgage, as recommended earlier in this chapter, may make better sense than investing in the stock market.

To determine your general investment preferences, think about how you would deal with an investment that plunges 20 percent, 40 percent, or more in a few years or less. Some aggressive investments can fall fast. You shouldn't go into the stock market, real estate, or small-business investment arena if such a drop is likely to cause you to sell low or make you a miserable, anxious wreck. If you haven't tried riskier invest-ments yet, you may want to experiment a bit to see how you feel with your money invested in them.

 A simple way to mask the risk of volatile investments is to *diversify* your portfolio — that is, to put your money into different investments.

Retirement Accounts

Saving money is difficult for most people. Don't make a tough job impossible by forsaking the tax benefits that come from investing through most retirement accounts.

Tax benefits

Retirement accounts should be called "tax-reduction accounts" — if they were, more people would be more moti-vated to contribute to them. Contributions to these plans are generally deductible for both your federal and state income taxes. Suppose you pay about 35 percent between federal and state income taxes on your last dollars of income. (See the section "Tax brackets" later in this chapter.) With most of the retirement accounts that I describe in this chapter, you can save yourself about $350 in taxes for every $1,000 that you contribute in the year that you make your contribution.

After your money is in a retirement account, any interest, dividends, and appreciation grow inside the account without taxation. With most retirement accounts, you defer taxes on all the accumulating gains and profits until you withdraw your money down the road, which you can do without penalty after age 59½. In the meantime, more of your money works for you over a long period of time. In some cases, such as with the Roth IRAs described later in this chapter, withdrawals are tax free, too.

Start saving sooner

A common mistake that many investors make is neglecting to take advantage of retirement accounts because of their enthusiasm to spend or invest in non-retirement accounts. Not investing in tax-sheltered retirement accounts can cost you hundreds, perhaps thousands, of dollars per year in lost tax savings. Add up that loss over the years that you work and save, and you find that not taking advantage of these tax-reduction accounts can cost you tens of thousands to hundreds of thousands of dollars in the long term.

To take advantage of retirement savings plans and the tax savings that accompany them, you must first spend less than you earn. Only then can you afford to contribute to these retirement savings plans.

 The sooner you start to save, the less painful it is each year to save enough to reach your goals. Why? Because your contributions have more years to compound.

Each decade you delay saving approximately doubles the percentage of your earnings that you need to save to meet your goals. For example, if saving 5 percent per year in your early 20s gets you to your retirement goal, waiting until your 30s to start may mean socking away 10 percent to reach that same goal; waiting until your 40s, 20 percent. Beyond that, the numbers get truly daunting.

Retirement account options

If you earn employment income (or receive alimony), you have options for putting money away in a retirement account that compounds without taxation until you withdraw the money.

In most cases, your contributions to these retirement accounts are tax deductible.

Company-based plans

If you work for a for-profit company, you may have access to a *401(k) plan*, which typically allows you to save up to $18,000 per year (for tax year 2017). Many nonprofit organizations offer *403(b) plans* to their employees. As with a 401(k), your contributions to a 403(b) plan are deductible on both your federal and state taxes in the year that you make them. Nonprofit employees can generally contribute up to 20 percent or $18,000 of their salaries, whichever is less. In addition to the upfront and ongoing tax benefits of these retirement savings plans, some employers match your contributions.

Older employees (defined as being at least age 50) can contribute even more into these company-based plans — up to $24,000 in 2017.

If you're self-employed, you can establish your own retirement savings plans for yourself and any employees you have. A *simplified employee pension individual retirement account (SEP-IRA)* allows you to sock away about 20 percent of your self-employment income (business revenue minus expenses), up to an annual maximum of $54,000 (for tax year 2017). Each year, *you* decide the amount you want to contribute — no minimums exist.

IRAs

If you work for a company that doesn't offer a retirement savings plan, or if you've exhausted contributing to your company's plan, consider an *individual retirement account* (IRA). Anyone with employment income (or who receives alimony) may contribute up to $5,500 each year to an IRA (or the amount of your employment or alimony income if it's less than $5,500 in a year). If you're a nonworking spouse, you're eligible to put up to $5,500 per year into a spousal IRA. Those age 50 and older can put away up to $6,500 per year (effective in 2017).

Your contributions to an IRA may or may not be tax deductible. For tax year 2017, if you're single and your adjusted gross income is $62,000 or less for the year, you can deduct your full IRA contribution. If you're married and you file your taxes jointly, you're entitled to a full IRA deduction if your AGI is $99,000 per year or less.

If you can't deduct your contribution to a standard IRA account, consider making a contribution to a non-deductible IRA account called the *Roth IRA*. Single taxpayers with an AGI less than $118,000 and joint filers with an AGI less than $186,000 can contribute up to $5,500 per year to a Roth IRA. Those age 50 and older can contribute $6,500. Although the contribution isn't deductible, earnings inside the account are shielded from taxes, and, unlike a standard IRA, qualified withdrawals from the account are free from income tax.

Retirement account investments

When you establish a retirement account, you may not realize that the retirement account is simply a shell or shield that keeps the federal, state, and local governments from taxing your investment earnings each year. You still must choose which investments you want to hold inside your retirement account shell.

You may invest money for your IRA or self-employed plan retirement account in stocks, bonds, mutual funds, exchange-traded funds, and even bank accounts. Mutual funds (offered in most employer-based plans), which I cover in detail in Chapters 9 and 10, are an ideal choice because they offer diversification and professional management. After you decide which financial institution you want to invest through, simply obtain and complete the appropriate paperwork for establishing the specific type of account you want.

Taxes and Non-Retirement Accounts

When you invest outside of tax-sheltered retirement accounts, the profits and distributions on your money are subject to taxation. So the non-retirement account investments that make sense for you depend (at least partly) on your tax situation.

If you have money to invest, or if you're considering selling current investments that you hold, taxes should factor into your decision. But tax considerations alone shouldn't dictate how and where you invest your money. You should also weigh investment choices, your desire and the necessity to take risk, personal likes and dislikes, and the number of years you plan to hold the investment (see the section "The Right Investment Mix," later in the chapter, for more information on these factors).

Tax brackets

You may not know it, but the government charges you different tax rates for different parts of your annual income. You pay less tax on the *first* dollars of your earnings and more tax on the *last* dollars of your earnings. For example, if you're single and your taxable income totaled $50,000 during 2017, you paid federal tax at the rate of 10 percent on the first $9,325, 15 percent on the taxable income above $9,325 up to $37,950, and 25 percent on income above $37,950 up to $50,000.

Your *marginal tax rate* is the rate of tax that you pay on your *last*, or so-called *highest*, dollars of income. In the example of a single person with taxable income of $50,000, that person's federal marginal tax rate is 25 percent. In other words, he effectively pays a 25 percent federal tax on his last dollars of income — those dollars earned between $37,950 and $50,000. (Don't forget to factor in the state income taxes that most states assess.)

_____

_____

_____

Knowing your marginal tax rate allows you to quickly calculate the following:

- Any additional taxes that you would pay on additional income

- The amount of taxes that you save if you contribute more money into retirement accounts or reduce your taxable income (for example, if you choose investments that produce tax-free income)

Table 3-1 shows the federal income tax rates for singles and for married households that file jointly.

Singles Taxable Income	Married Filing Jointly Taxable Income	Federal Tax Rate
Less than $9,325	Less than $18,650	10%
$9,326 to $37,950	$18,651 to $75,900	15%
$37,951 to $91,900	$75,901 to $153,100	25%
$91,901 to $191,650	$153,101 to $233,350	28%
$191,651 to $416,700	$233,351 to $416,700	33%
$416,701 to $418,400	$416,701 to $470,700	35%
More than $418,400	More than $470,700	39.6%

Table 3-1: *2017 Federal Income Tax Rates*

Knowing what's taxed

Interest you receive from bank accounts and corporate bonds is generally taxable. US Treasury bonds pay interest that's state-tax-free. Municipal bonds, which state and local governments issue, pay interest that's federal-tax-free and also state-tax-free to residents in the state where the bond is issued. (I discuss bonds in Chapters 7 and 8.)

Taxation on your *capital gains,* which is the *profit* (sales minus purchase price) on an investment, works under a unique system. Investments held less than one year generate *short-term capital gains,* which are taxed at your normal marginal rate. Profits from investments that you hold longer than 12 months are *long-term capital gains.* These long-term gains cap at 20 percent, which is the rate that applies only for those in the highest federal income tax bracket of 39.6 percent. The long-term capital gains tax rate is just 15 percent for everyone else, except for those in the two lowest income tax brackets of 10 and 15 percent. For these folks, the long-term capital gains tax rate is 0 percent.

_____

_____

_____

Use these strategies to reduce the taxes you pay on investments that are exposed to taxation:

- **Opt for tax-free money markets and bonds.** If you're in a high enough tax bracket, you may find that you come out ahead with tax-free investments. Tax-free investments yield less than comparable investments that produce taxable earnings, but because of the tax differences, the earnings from tax-free investments *can* end up being greater than what taxable investments leave you with. To compare properly, subtract what you'll pay in federal as well as state taxes from the taxable investment to see which investment nets you more.

- **Invest in tax-friendly stock funds.** Mutual and exchange-traded funds that tend to trade less tend to produce lower capital gains distributions. For funds held outside tax-sheltered retirement accounts, this reduced trading effectively increases an investor's total rate of return. *Index funds* invest in a relatively static portfolio of securities, such as stocks and bonds. They don't attempt to beat the market. Rather, they invest in the securities to mirror or match the performance of an underlying index, such as the Standard & Poor's 500. Although index funds can't beat the market, the typical actively managed fund doesn't either, and index funds have several advantages over actively managed funds.

Short-term capital gains (investments held one year or less) are taxed at your ordinary income tax rate. This is another reason you shouldn't trade your investments quickly (within 12 months).

The Right Investment Mix

Diversifying your investments helps buffer your portfolio from being sunk by one or two poor performers. In the following sections, I explain how to choose a smart mix of investments.

Consider your age

When you're younger and have more years until you plan to use your money, you should keep larger amounts of your long-term investment money in *growth* (ownership) vehicles, such as stocks, real estate, and small business. As I discuss in Chapter 2, the attraction of these types of investments is the potential to really grow your money. The risk: The value of your portfolio can fall from time to time.

The younger you are, the more time your investments have to recover from a bad fall. A long-held guiding principle says to subtract your age from 110 and invest the resulting number as a percentage of money to place in growth (ownership) investments. So if you're 35 years old:

$110 - 35 = 75$ percent of your investment money can be in growth investments

If you want to be more aggressive, subtract your age from 120:

$120 - 35 = 85$ percent of your investment money can be in growth investments

Retired people should still have a healthy chunk of their investment dollars in growth vehicles like stocks. A 70-year-old person may want to totally avoid risk, but doing so is generally a mistake. Such a person can live another two or three decades. If you live longer than anticipated, you can run out of money if it doesn't continue to grow.

These tips are only general guidelines and apply to money that you invest for the long term (ideally for ten years or more).

For money that you need to use in the shorter term, such as within the next several years, more-aggressive growth investments aren't appropriate.

Make the most of your investment options

No hard-and-fast rules dictate how to allocate the percentage that you've earmarked for growth among specific investments like stocks. Part of how you decide to allocate your investments depends on the types of investments that you want to focus on. As I discuss in Chapter 4, diversifying in stocks worldwide can be prudent as well as profitable.

Here are some general guidelines to keep in mind:

- **Take advantage of your retirement accounts.** Unless you need accessible money for shorter-term non-retirement goals, why pass up the free extra returns from the tax benefits of retirement accounts?

- **Don't pile your money into investments that have gained lots of attention.** Many investors make this mistake, especially those who lack a thought-out plan to buy stocks.

- **Have the courage to be a contrarian.** No one likes to feel that he is jumping on board a sinking ship or supporting a losing cause. However, just as in shopping for something at retail stores, the best time to buy something of quality is when its price is reduced.

- **Diversify.** As I discuss in Chapter 2, the values of different investments don't move in tandem. So when you invest in growth investments, such as stocks, your portfolio's value will have a smoother ride if you diversify properly.

- **Invest more in what you know.** Over the years, I've met successful investors who have built substantial wealth without spending gobs of their free time researching, selecting, and monitoring investments. No one-size-fits-all code exists for successful investors. Just be careful that you don't put all of your investing eggs in the same basket.

- **Don't invest in too many different things.** Diversification is good to a point. But if you purchase so many investments that you can't perform a basic annual review of all of them (for example, reading the annual reports from your mutual and exchange-traded funds), you have too many investments.

- **Be more aggressive with investments inside retirement accounts.** When you hit your retirement years, you'll probably begin to live off your non-retirement account investments first. Allowing your retirement accounts to continue to grow can generally save you tax dollars. Therefore, you should be relatively less aggressive with investments outside of retirement accounts because that money may be invested for a shorter time period.

Dollar cost averaging

Dollar cost averaging (DCA) is the practice of investing a regular amount of money at set time intervals, such as monthly or quarterly, into volatile investments, such as stocks and stock mutual funds. If you've ever had money deducted from your paycheck and invested it into a retirement savings plan investment account that holds stocks and bonds, you've done DCA.

Most people invest a portion of their employment compensation as they earn it, but if you have extra cash sitting around, you can choose to invest that money in one fell swoop or to invest it gradually via DCA. The biggest appeal of gradually feeding money into the market via DCA is that you don't dump all your money into a potentially overheated investment just before a major drop. Thus, DCA helps shy investors psychologically ease into riskier investments.

DCA is made to order for skittish investors with large lump sums of money sitting in safe investments like CDs or savings accounts. For example, using DCA, an investor with $100,000 to invest in stock funds can feed her money into investments gradually — say, at the rate of $12,500 or so quarterly over two years — instead of investing her entire $100,000 in stocks at once and possibly buying all of her shares at or near a market peak. Most large investment companies, especially mutual funds, allow investors to establish automatic investment plans so the DCA occurs without an investor's ongoing involvement.

Of course, like any risk-reducing investment strategy, DCA has drawbacks. If growth investments appreciate (as they're supposed to), a DCA investor misses out on earning higher returns on his money awaiting investment.

Apprehensive investors who shun lump-sum investments and use DCA are more likely to stop the DCA investment process if prices plunge, thereby defeating the benefit of doing DCA during a declining market.

_____

_____

_____

So what's an investor with a lump sum of money to do?

- **First, weigh the significance of the lump sum to you.** Although $100,000 is a big chunk of most people's net worth, it's only 10 percent if your net worth is $1,000,000. It's not worth a millionaire's time to use DCA for $100,000. If the cash you have to invest is less than a quarter of your net worth, you may not want to bother with DCA.

- **Second, consider how aggressively you invest (or invested) your money.** For example, if you aggressively invested your money through an employer's retirement plan that you roll over, don't waste your time on DCA.

As for the times of the year that you should use DCA, mutual fund and exchange-traded fund investors should use DCA early in each calendar quarter because funds that make taxable distributions tend to do so late in the quarter.

 Your money that awaits investment in DCA should have a suitable parking place. Select a high-yielding money market fund that's appropriate for your tax situation.

_____

_____

_____

One last critical point: When you use DCA, establish an automatic investment plan so you're less likely to chicken out.

Investing for College

Many well-intentioned parents want to save for their children's future educational expenses. The mistake they often make, however, is putting money in accounts in their child's name (in so-called *custodial accounts*) or saving outside of retirement accounts in general.

The more money you accumulate outside tax-sheltered retirement accounts, the less assistance you're likely to qualify for from federal and state financial aid sources. Don't make the additional error of assuming that financial aid is only for the poor. Many middle-income and even some modestly affluent families qualify for some aid, which can include grants and loans, even if you're not deemed financially needy.

Under the current financial needs analysis that most colleges use in awarding financial aid, the value of your retirement plan is *not* considered an asset. Money that you save *outside* of retirement accounts, including money in the child's name, is counted as an asset and reduces eligibility for financial aid.

> Don't forgo contributing to your own retirement savings plan(s) in order to save money in a non-retirement account for your children's college expenses. When you do, you pay higher taxes both on your current income and on the interest and growth of this money. In addition to paying higher taxes, you're expected to contribute more to your child's educational expenses (because you'll receive less financial aid).

If you plan to apply for financial aid, it's a good idea to save non-retirement account money in your name rather than in your child's name (as a custodial account). Colleges expect a greater percentage of money in your child's name (35 percent) to be used for college costs than money in your name (6 percent). Remember, though, that from the standpoint of getting financial aid, you're better off saving inside retirement accounts.

Education Savings Accounts

Be careful about funding an Education Savings Account (ESA). In theory, an ESA sounds like a great place to park some college savings. Subject to income limitations, you can make non-deductible contributions of up to $2,000 per child per year, and investment earnings and account withdrawals are free of tax as long as you use the funds to pay for elementary and secondary school or college costs. However, funding an ESA can undermine your child's ability to qualify for financial aid. It's best to keep the parents as the owners of such an account for financial aid purposes, but be forewarned that some schools may treat money in an ESA as a student's asset.

Section 529 plans

Also known as *qualified state tuition plans*, Section 529 plans offer a tax-advantaged way to save and invest more than $100,000 per child toward college costs (some states allow upward of $300,000 per student). After you contribute to one of these state-based accounts, the invested funds grow without taxation. Withdrawals are also tax-free so long as the funds are used to pay for qualifying higher educational costs (which include college, graduate school, and certain additional expenses of special-needs students). The schools need not be in the same state as the state administering the Section 529 plan.

As I discuss in the preceding section about Education Savings Accounts, Section 529 plan balances can harm your child's financial aid chances. Thus, such accounts make the most sense for affluent families who are sure that they won't qualify for any type of financial aid. If you do opt for an ESA and intend to apply for financial aid, you should be the owner of the accounts (not your child) to maximize qualifying for financial aid.

_____

_____

_____

4

Building Wealth
with Stocks

Shares of stock, which represent portions of ownership in companies, offer a way for people of modest and wealthy means, and everybody in between, to invest in companies and build wealth. History shows that long-term investors can win in the stock market because it appreciates over the years. That said, some people who remain active in the market over many years manage to lose some money because of easily avoidable mistakes. This chapter gets you up to speed on successful stock market investing.

Making Money with Stocks

When you purchase a share of a company's stock, you can profit from your ownership in two ways:

- **Dividends:** Most stocks pay dividends. Companies generally make some profits during the year. Some high-growth companies reinvest most or all of their profits right back into the business. Many companies, however, pay out some of their profits to shareholders in the form of quarterly *dividends*.

- **Appreciation:** When the price per share of your stock rises to a level greater than you originally paid for it, you make money. This profit, however, is only on paper until you sell the stock, at which time you realize a *capital gain*. (Such gains realized over periods longer than one year are taxed at the lower long-term capital gains tax rate; see Chapter 3.) Of course, the stock price per share can fall below what you originally paid as well (in which case you have a loss on paper unless you realize that loss by selling).

If you add together dividends and appreciation, you arrive at your total return. Stocks differ in the dimensions of these possible returns, particularly with respect to dividends.

Defining "the Market"

You invest in stocks to share in the rewards of capitalistic economies. When you invest in stocks, you do so through the stock market. What is the stock market? People talk about "the Market" the same way they do the largest city nearby ("the City"):

The Market is down 137 points today.

With the Market hitting new highs, isn't now a bad time to invest?

The Market seems ready for a fall.

When people talk about the Market, they're usually referring to the US stock market. Even more specifically, they're usually speaking about the *Dow Jones Industrial Average*, created by Charles Dow and Eddie Jones, which is a widely watched index or measure of the performance of the US stock market. Dow and Jones, two reporters, started publishing *The*

Wall Street Journal in 1889. Like the modern-day version, the nineteenth-century *Wall Street Journal* reported current financial news. Dow and Jones also compiled stock prices of larger, important companies and created and calculated indexes to track the performance of the US stock market.

The Dow Jones Industrial Average ("the Dow") market index tracks the performance of 30 large companies that are headquartered in the United States. The Dow 30 includes companies such as telecommunications giant Verizon; airplane manufacturer Boeing; beverage maker Coca-Cola; oil giant Exxon Mobil; technology behemoths Apple and Microsoft; drug makers Merck and Pfizer; fast-food king McDonald's; and retailers Home Depot and Wal-Mart.

Major stock market indexes

Just as New York City isn't the only city to visit or live in, the 30 stocks in the Dow Jones Industrial Average are far from representative of all the different types of stocks you can invest in. Here are some other important market indexes and the types of stocks they track:

- **Standard & Poor's (S&P) 500:** Like the Dow Jones Industrial Average, the S&P 500 tracks the price of 500 larger-company US stocks. These 500 big companies account for more than 70 percent of the total market value of the tens of thousands of stocks traded in the United States. Thus, the S&P 500 is a much broader and more representative index of the larger-company stocks in the United States than the Dow Jones Industrial Average is.

- **Russell 2000:** This index tracks the market value of 2,000 smaller US company stocks of various industries. Although small-company stocks tend to move in tandem with larger-company stocks over the longer term, it's not unusual for one to rise or fall more than the other or for one index to fall while the other rises in a given year. For example, in 2001, the Russell 2000 actually rose 2.5 percent while the S&P 500 fell 11.9 percent. In 2007, the Russell 2000 lost 1.6 percent versus a gain of 5.5 percent for the S&P 500. Be aware that smaller-company stocks tend to be more volatile. (Turn to Chapter 2 for information about risks and returns.)

- **Wilshire 5000:** Despite its name, the Wilshire 5000 index actually tracks the prices of more than 5,000 stocks of US companies of all sizes — small, medium, and large.

Thus, many consider this index the broadest and most representative of the overall US stock market.

- **MSCI EAFE:** Stocks don't exist only in the United States. MSCI's EAFE index tracks the prices of stocks in the other major developed countries of the world. *EAFE* stands for Europe, Australasia, and Far East.

- **MSCI Emerging Markets:** This index follows the value of stocks in the less economically developed but "emerging" countries, such as Brazil, China, Russia, Taiwan, India, South Africa, Chile, Mexico, and so on. These stock markets tend to be more volatile than those in established economies. During good economic times, emerging markets usually reward investors with higher returns, but stocks can fall farther and faster than stocks in developed markets.

Conspicuously absent from this list of major stock market indexes is the NASDAQ index. With the boom in technology stock prices in the late 1990s, CNBC and other financial media started broadcasting movements in the technology-laden NASDAQ index, thereby increasing investor interest and the frenzy surrounding technology stocks. I'm not a fan of sector (industry) specific investing because it undermines diversification. I suggest ignoring industry-concentrated indexes.

Using indexes

Indexes serve several purposes. First, they can quickly give you an idea of how particular types of stocks perform in comparison with other types of stocks. In 1998, for example, the S&P 500 was up 28.6 percent, whereas the small-company Russell 2000 index was down 2.5 percent. That same year, the MSCI foreign stock EAFE index rose 20.3 percent. In 2001, by contrast, the S&P 500 fell 11.9 percent, and the EAFE foreign stock index had an even worse year, falling 21.4 percent. In 2013, the S&P 500 surged 29.7 percent while the foreign EAFE index returned 18 percent.

Indexes also allow you to compare or benchmark the performance of your stock market investments. If you invest primarily in large-company US stocks, for example, you should compare the overall return of the stocks in your portfolio to a comparable index — in this case, the S&P 500. (As I discuss in Chapter 9, *index mutual funds*, which invest to match a major stock market index, offer a cost-effective, proven way to build wealth by investing in stocks.)

You may also hear about some other types of more narrowly focused indexes, including those that track the performance of stocks in particular industries, such as advertising, banking, computers, pharmaceuticals, restaurants, semiconductors, textiles, and utilities. Other indexes cover the stock markets of other countries, such as the United Kingdom, Germany, France, Canada, and Hong Kong.

Focusing your investments in the stocks of just one or two industries or smaller countries is dangerous due to the lack of diversification and your lack of expertise in making the difficult decision about what to invest in and when. Thus, I suggest that you ignore these narrower indexes.

Stock-Buying Methods

When you invest in stocks, many choices exist. Besides the tens of thousands of stocks from which you can select, you also can invest in mutual funds or exchange-traded funds (ETFs) or you can have a stockbroker select for you.

_____

_____

_____

Buying stocks via mutual funds and exchange-traded funds

If you're busy and suffer no delusions about your expertise, you'll love the best stock mutual funds. Investing in stocks through mutual funds can be as simple as dialing a toll-free phone number or logging on to a fund company's website, completing some application forms, and sending it some money.

Mutual funds take money invested by people like you and me and pool it in a single investment portfolio in securities, such as stocks and bonds. The portfolio is then professionally managed. Stock mutual funds, as the name suggests, invest primarily or exclusively in stocks (some stock funds sometimes invest a bit in other stuff, such as bonds).

Exchange-traded funds (ETFs) are in many ways similar to mutual funds, specifically index funds (see Chapter 9), except that they trade on a stock exchange. One potential attraction is that some ETFs offer investors the potential for even lower operating expenses than comparable mutual funds and may be tax friendlier. I expand on ETFs in Chapters 9 and 10.

Stock funds include many advantages:

- **Diversification:** Buying individual stocks on your own is relatively costly unless you buy reasonable chunks (100 shares or so) of each stock. But to buy 100 shares each in, say, a dozen companies' stocks to ensure diversification, you need about $60,000 if the stocks you buy average $50 per share.

- **Professional management:** Even if you have big bucks to invest, funds offer something that you can't deliver: professional, full-time management. Fund managers peruse a company's financial statements and otherwise track and analyze its business strategy and market position. The best managers put in long hours and possess lots of expertise and experience in the field. Funds are a huge timesaver for individual investors.

- **Low costs — if you pick 'em right:** Some funds are expensive, charging you a couple percent or more per year in operating expenses on top of hefty sales commissions.

  But just as you wouldn't want to invest in a fund that a novice with no track record manages, why would you want to invest in a high-cost fund? Contrary to the "You get what you pay for" notion often trumpeted by those trying to sell you something at an inflated price, some of the best managers are the cheapest to hire. Through a *no-load* (commission-free) mutual fund, you can hire a professional, full-time money manager to invest $10,000 for a mere $20 to $100 per year. Some index funds and exchange-traded funds charge even less.

As with all investments, funds have some drawbacks. Consider the following:

- **The issue of control is a problem for some investors.** If you like being in control, sending your investment dollars to a seemingly black-box process where others decide when and in what to invest your money may unnerve you. However, you need to be more concerned about the potential missteps that you may make investing in individual stocks of your own choosing or those stocks pitched to you by a broker.

- **Taxes are a concern when you invest in funds outside of retirement accounts.** Because the fund manager decides when to sell specific stock holdings, some funds may produce relatively high levels of taxable distributions. Fear not — simply select tax-friendly funds if taxes concern you.

Selecting individual stocks yourself

More than a few investing books encourage people to do their own stock picking. However, the vast majority of investors are better off *not* picking their own stocks in my observations and experience.

I've long been an advocate of educating yourself and taking responsibility for your own financial affairs, but taking responsibility for your finances doesn't mean you should do *everything* yourself. Table 4-1 includes some thoughts to consider about choosing your own stocks.

Good Reasons to Pick Your Own Stocks	Bad Reasons to Pick Your Own Stocks
You enjoy the challenge.	You think you can beat the best money managers.
You want to learn more about business.	You want more control over your investments, which you think may happen if you understand the companies you invest in.
You possess a substantial amount of money to invest.	You think that mutual funds are for people who aren't smart enough to choose their own stocks.
You're a buy-and-hold investor.	You're attracted to the ability to trade your stocks anytime you want.

Table 4-1: *Why You're Buying Your Own Stocks*

Some popular investing books try to convince investors that they can do a *better* job than the professionals at picking their own stocks. Amateur investors, however, need to devote a lot of study to become proficient at stock selection. Many professional investors work 80 hours a week at investing, but you're unlikely to be willing to spend that much time on it. Don't let the popularity of those do-it-yourself stock-picking books lead you astray.

Choosing a stock isn't as simple as visiting a restaurant chain, liking it, buying its stock, and then sitting back and getting rich watching your stock zoom to the moon.

If you invest in stocks, you probably know by now that guarantees don't exist. But as in many of life's endeavors, you can buy individual stocks in good and not-so-good ways. If you want to select your own individual stocks, check out Chapters 5 and 6, where I explain how to best research and trade them.

Keys to Stock Market Success

Anybody, no matter what his or her educational background, IQ, occupation, income, or assets, can make solid returns through stock investments. Over long periods of time, based on historic performance, you can expect to earn an average of about 9 percent per year total return by investing in stocks.

 To maximize your chances of stock market investment success, do the following:

- **Don't try to time the markets.** Anticipating where the stock market and specific stocks are heading is next to impossible. Economic factors, which are influenced by thousands of elements, determine stock market prices. Be a regular buyer of stocks with new savings. Consider buying more stocks when they're on sale and market pessimism is running high. Don't make the mistake of bailing out when the market is down!

- **Diversify your investments.** Invest in the stocks of different-sized companies in varying industries around the world. When assessing your investments' performance, examine your whole portfolio at least once a year and calculate your total return after expenses and trading fees.

- **Keep trading costs, management fees, and commissions to a minimum.** These costs represent a big drain on your returns. If you invest through an individual broker or a financial advisor who earns a living on commissions, odds are that you're paying more than you need to be. And you're likely receiving biased advice, too.

- **Pay attention to taxes.** Like commissions and fees, federal and state taxes are a major investment "expense" that you can minimize. Contribute most of your money to your tax-advantaged retirement accounts. You can invest your money outside of retirement accounts, but keep an eye on taxes (see Chapter 3). Calculate your annual returns on an *after*-tax basis.

- **Don't overestimate your ability to pick the big-winning stocks.** One of the best ways to invest in stocks is through mutual funds and exchange-traded funds (see Chapters 9 and 10), which allow you to use an experienced, full-time money manager at a low cost to perform all the investing grunt work for you.

5

Researching Stocks

This chapter provides a crash course in researching individual companies and their stocks. Be sure you consider your reasons for taking this approach before you head down the path of picking and choosing your own stocks. Take a look at Chapter 6 to better understand the process of purchasing stocks on your own.

If you decide to tackle the task of researching your own stocks, you don't have to worry about finding enough information: The problem to worry about is information overload. You can literally spend hundreds of hours researching and reading information on one company alone. Therefore, you need to focus on where you can get the best return for your time and money.

Building on Others' Research

When deciding which stocks to invest in, you have a wealth of information to draw from. However, you don't have to sort through the numbers and analyses on your own. You can lean on the insights of industry experts. In the following sections, I highlight useful resources that provide valuable information when you're trying to pick the best stocks.

Independent brokerage research

If you're going to invest in individual stocks, you need a brokerage account. In addition to offering low trading fees, the best brokerage firms allow you to easily tap into useful research, especially through the firm's website, that you can use to assist you with your investing decisions.

Because discount brokers aren't in the investment banking business of working with companies to sell new issues of stock, discount brokers have a level of objectivity in their research reports that traditional brokers (like Merrill Lynch, Morgan Stanley, and so on) too often lack. Some discount brokers, such as Charles Schwab, produce their own research reports, but most discount brokers simply provide reports from independent third parties. See Chapter 11 for how to select a top-notch brokerage firm.

Money managers' stock picks

To make money in stocks, you certainly don't need an original idea. In fact, it makes sense to examine what the best money managers are buying for their portfolios.

Mutual fund managers, for example, are required to disclose at least twice a year what stocks they hold in their portfolio. You can call the best fund companies and ask them to send their most recent semiannual reports that detail their stock holdings, or you can view those reports on many fund companies' websites.

Through its website, Morningstar (www.morningstar.com) allows you to see which mutual funds hold large portions of a given stock that you may be researching and what the success or lack thereof is of the funds that are buying a given stock.

Finally, you can follow what investment legend Warren Buffett is buying through his holding company, Berkshire Hathaway. If you'd like to review Berkshire's complete corporate filings on your own, visit the Securities and Exchange Commission website at www.sec.gov.

Financial publications and websites

Many publications and websites cover the world of stocks. But you have to be careful. Just because certain columnists or publications advocate particular stocks or investing strategies doesn't mean you'll achieve success by following their advice.

The following publications offer useful columns and commentary, sometimes written by professional money managers, on individual stocks: *Barron's, Bloomberg Business Week, Forbes, Kiplinger's,* and *The Wall Street Journal.* In addition, hundreds of websites are devoted to stock picking.

Annual Reports

All publicly traded companies must annually file certain financial documents. When you've identified a company whose stock you want to purchase, consider reviewing these documents to enhance your understanding of the company's businesses and strategies rather than for the predictive value that you may hope they provide.

The first of such useful documents that companies produce is the *annual report.* This yearly report provides standardized financial statements as well as management's discussion about how the company has performed and how it plans to improve its performance in the future. If you're the skeptical sort, you may think, "Aren't the company's officials going to make everything sound rosy?"

To a certain extent, yes, but not as badly as you may think, especially at companies that adhere to sound accounting principles and good old-fashioned ethics. First, a large portion of annual reports include the company's financial statements, which an accounting firm must audit. However, audits don't mean that companies and their accounting firms can't (often legally) structure the company's books to make them look rosier than they really are. And some companies have pulled the wool over the eyes of their auditors, who then become unwitting accomplices in producing false financial figures.

Also keep in mind that more than a few companies have been sued for misleading shareholders with inflated forecasts or lack of disclosure of problems. Responsible companies try to present a balanced and, of course, hopeful perspective in their annual reports. Most companies' annual reports are also written by non-techno geeks, so you have a decent chance of understanding them.

The following sections walk you through the three main elements of the standard annual report: financial and business highlights, the balance sheet, and the income statement.

Financial and business highlights

The first section of most annual reports presents a description of a company's recent financial highlights and business strategies. You can use this information to find out about the businesses that the company is in and where the company is heading.

Balance sheet

You can find a company's hard-core financials in the back portion of most annual reports. (You can find many of these same numbers in *Value Line Investment Survey* reports, but you get more specific details in the company's annual report.) All annual reports contain a *balance sheet*, which is a snapshot summary of all the company's *assets* (what the company owns) and *liabilities* (what the company owes). The balance sheet covers the company's assets and liabilities from the beginning of the year to the last day of the company's year-end, which is typically December 31. Some companies use a fiscal year that ends at other times of the year.

A company's balance sheet resembles a personal balance sheet. The entries, of course, look a little different because you likely don't own things like manufacturing equipment.

Assets

The assets section of the balance sheet lists the following items that a company holds or owns that are of significant value:

- **Cash:** Companies invest their cash to earn interest. Explanatory notes often follow the balance sheet to explain certain items in more detail.

- **Accounts receivable:** This item represents money that is owed to the company, such as customer invoices that haven't been paid yet.

  As companies grow, their accounts receivable usually do, too. Watch out for cases where the receivables grow faster than the sales (revenue). This growth may indicate that the company is having problems with its products' quality or pricing. Unhappy customers pay more slowly or demand bigger price discounts.

- **Investments:** In addition to cash, some companies may invest in other securities, such as bonds and stocks. Just as with your own personal situation, companies usually invest money that they don't expect to use in the near future.

- **Property and equipment:** All companies need equipment to run their businesses. This equipment can include office furniture, computers, real estate they own, and manufacturing machinery that companies use to make their products. Equipment becomes less valuable over time, so a company must consider this depreciation as a cost of doing business each year. Therefore, if a company ceases buying new equipment, this entry on the balance sheet gradually decreases because the company continues to subtract the depreciation from the value of the equipment.

- **Goodwill:** One of the assets that doesn't show up on most companies' balance sheets is their *goodwill*. Companies work hard through advertising, product development, and service to attract and retain customers and to build *name-brand recognition*.

_____

_____

_____

Companies can't put a value on the goodwill that they've generated, but when they purchase (acquire) another firm, some of the purchase price is considered goodwill. Specifically, if a company is acquired for $100 million but has a *net worth* (assets minus liabilities) of just $50 million, the extra $50 million goes to goodwill. The goodwill then becomes an asset on the acquiring company's balance sheet.

- **Other assets:** This catch-all category may include some stuff that can make your eyes glaze over. For example, companies keep a different set of books for tax purposes (yes, this is legal). Not surprisingly, companies do so because the IRS allows, in some cases, more deductions than what the company is required to show from an accounting standpoint on its financial statements. (If you were a company, wouldn't you want your shareholders, but not the IRS, to see gobs of profits?) Companies treat tax deferment as an asset until the IRS receives more of its share down the road.

Manufacturing and retail companies also track and report *inventory* (the product that hasn't yet been sold) as an asset. Generally speaking, as a business grows, so does its inventory. If inventory grows more quickly than revenue, such growth may be a warning sign. This growth can indicate that customers are scaling back purchases and that the company miscalculated and overproduced. It can also be a leading indicator of an obsolete or inferior product offering.

Liabilities

This section of the balance sheet summarizes all the money that a company owes to other entities:

- **Accounts payable:** When a company places orders to purchase things for its business, it sometimes has a lag between receiving a bill and paying it; the money owed is called *accounts payable.* As with inventory and accounts receivable, accounts payable generally increases with a company's increasing revenue.

  If accounts payable increases faster than revenue, the company may have a problem. On the other hand, that increase can also be a sign of good financial management. The longer you take to pay your bills, the longer you have the money in your pocket working for you.

- **Accrued compensation:** This line tallies money that the company must someday pay its employees. For example, many larger firms maintain pension plans. These plans promise workers who retire with at least five years of service a monthly income check in retirement. Thus, the company must reserve this money that it owes and list it as a liability or debt that it must someday pay.

- **Income taxes payable:** Companies are in business to make a profit, and as they earn those profits, they need to reserve a portion to pay income taxes. As I explain in the preceding section, some of the taxes that the company owes can be the result of accounting differences between the company's financial statements and those filed with the IRS.

- **Dividends payable:** Not all companies pay dividends (see Chapter 4) to their shareholders. But those companies that do pay dividends typically declare the dividend several weeks in advance of when they actually owe the dividend. During this interim period, the company lists the not-yet-paid dividends as a liability.

_____

_____

_____

Stockholders' equity

The difference between a company's assets and liabilities is known as *stockholders' equity*. Stockholders' equity is what makes balance sheets always balance.

Income statement

The other big financial statement in an annual report is the income statement. I discuss the elements of a corporate income statement next.

Revenue

Revenue is simply the money that a company receives from its customers as compensation for its products or services. Just as you can earn income from your job(s) as well as from investments and other sources, a company can make money from a variety of sources. In the case of mutual fund provider T. Rowe Price, the firm collects fees (investment advisory and administrative) for the mutual fund investments that it manages on behalf of its customers as well as privately managed money for wealthy individuals and institutions. The company also receives income from its own money that it has invested.

Ideally, you want to see a steady or accelerating rate of growth in a company's revenue. If a company's revenue grows more slowly, you need to inquire why. Is it because of poor service or product performance, better competitor offerings, ineffective marketing, or all of the above?

For companies with multiple divisions or product lines, the annual report may detail the revenue of each product line in a later section. Examine what spurs or holds back the company's overall growth and which different businesses the company operates in. Look for businesses that were acquired but don't really fit with the company's other business units as a red flag. Large companies that have experienced stalled revenue growth sometimes try to enter new businesses through acquisition but then don't manage them well because they don't understand the keys to their success.

When researching retail stores, such as restaurant chains (for example, McDonald's) or clothing stores (for example, The Gap), examine the revenue changes that come from opening new locations versus the changes at existing locations, sometimes referred to as *same stores*. Be concerned if you find that a company's revenue growth comes from opening new locations rather than growth at existing locations. This situation may indicate that opening more locations is masking weakness in the company's business.

Expenses

Just as personal income taxes and housing, food, and clothing expenses gobble up much of your personal income, company expenses use up much, and sometimes all, of a company's revenue.

Even healthy, growing businesses can get into trouble if their expenses grow faster than their revenues. Well-managed companies stay on top of their expenses during good and bad times. Unfortunately, it's easy for companies to get sloppy during good times.

It's particularly useful to examine each category of expenses relative to (in other words, as a percentage of) the company's revenue to see which ones grow or shrink. As a well-managed and financially healthy company grows, expenses as a percentage of revenue should decrease. In turn, profits as a percentage of revenue increase.

T. Rowe Price's total operating expenses relative to total revenues have increased, while profits (net operating income) relative to total revenues have decreased. Not all expense categories necessarily increase.

Net income calculations

The net result of expenses that increase more slowly than revenues is a fatter bottom line. Sometimes companies experience one-time events, such as the sale of a division, which can change profits temporarily. Companies usually list these one-time events in the section under expenses.

I encourage you to review the company's statement of cash flows included in its annual report. Cash can flow into and out of a company from normal business operations, investment activities, and financing activities. Sometimes a company may report higher profits but actually be facing decreased cash flow from operations — for example, if its customers are getting slower with paying bills (which could indicate that its customers are having financial problems or that they're unhappy with the product or service being provided).

Earnings per share

Last but not least, and of great importance to shareholders, is the calculation of earnings per share. Higher profits per share generally help fuel a higher stock price, and declining profits feed falling stock prices. Remember, though, that smart financial market participants are looking ahead, so if you run out to buy stock in a company that's reporting higher profits, those higher profits are old news and likely have already been priced into the company's current market value.

6

Purchasing Stocks

When investing in stocks, you're searching for a company that will be profitable and see its stock price increase. If it pays out dividends in the process, even better.

This chapter helps you understand how to compare companies' stock prices, read a stock table, and make your purchase.

The Right Times to Buy

After you know about the different types of stock markets and ways to invest in stocks, you may wonder how you can build wealth with stocks and not lose your shirt. Nobody wants to buy stocks before a big drop.

The stock market is reasonably efficient. A company's stock price normally reflects many smart people's assessments as to what is a fair price. Thus, it's not realistic for an investor to expect to discover a system for how to "buy low and sell high." Some professional investors may be able to spot good times to buy and sell particular stocks, but consistently doing so is enormously difficult.

The simplest and best way to make money in the stock market is to consistently and regularly feed new money into building a diversified and larger portfolio. If the market drops, you can use your new investment dollars to buy more shares. The danger of trying to time the market is that you may be "out" of the market when it appreciates greatly and "in" the market when it plummets.

Price-earnings ratios

Suppose the stock for Liz's Distinctive Jewelry sells for $50 per share and that another stock in the same industry, The Jazzy Jeweler, sells for $100. Which would you rather buy?

If you answer, "I don't know because I don't have enough information," you're correct. On its own, the price per share of stock is meaningless. Although The Jazzy Jeweler sells for twice as much per share, its profits may also be twice as much per share — in which case The Jazzy Jeweler stock price may not be out of line given its profitability.

The level of a company's stock price relative to its earnings or profits per share helps you calibrate how expensively, cheaply, or fairly a stock price is valued.

$$\frac{\text{Stock price per share}}{\text{Annual earnings per share}} = \text{Price-earnings (P/E) ratio}$$

Over the long term, stock prices and corporate profits tend to move in sync. The *price-earnings ratio*, or P/E ratio, compares the level of stock prices to the level of corporate profits, giving you a good sense of the stock's value. Over shorter periods of time, investors' emotions as well as fundamentals move stocks, but over longer terms, fundamentals possess a far greater influence on stock prices.

P/E ratios can be calculated for individual stocks as well as entire stock indexes, portfolios, or funds.

Over the past 100-plus years, the P/E ratio of US stocks has averaged around 15. During times of low inflation, the ratio tends to be higher — in the high teens to low 20s. In 1999, the P/E ratio for US stocks got into the 30s, well above historic norms even for a period of low inflation. Thus, the down market that began in 2000 wasn't surprising, especially given the fall in corporate profits that put even more pressure on stock prices.

Just because US stocks have historically averaged P/E ratios of about 15 doesn't mean that every individual stock will trade at such a P/E. Here's why: Suppose you have a choice between investing in two companies, Superb Software and Tortoise Technologies. Say both companies' stocks sell at a P/E of 15. If Superb Software's business and profits grow 40 percent per year and Tortoise's business and profits remain flat, which would you buy?

Because both stocks trade at a P/E of 15, Superb Software appears to be the better buy. Even if Superb's stock continues to sell at 15 times its earnings, its stock price should increase 40 percent per year as its profits increase. Faster-growing companies usually command higher price-earnings ratios.

Just because a stock price or an entire country's stock market seems to be at a high price level doesn't necessarily mean that that particular stock or market is overpriced. Always compare the price of a stock to that company's profits per share or the overall market's price level to the overall corporate profits. The price-earnings ratio captures this comparison. Faster-growing and more-profitable companies generally sell for a premium — they have higher P/E ratios. Also remember that future earnings, which are difficult to predict, influence stock prices more than current earnings, which are old news. Finally, keep in mind that a relatively low P/E ratio on a particular stock could be a possible warning sign of problems ahead.

When stocks go "on sale"

Along with speculative buying frenzies come valleys of pessimism when stock prices are falling sharply. Having the courage to buy when stock prices are "on sale" can pay big returns.

In the early 1970s, interest rates and inflation escalated. Oil prices shot up as an oil embargo choked off supplies, and Americans had to wait in long lines for gas. Gold prices soared, and the US dollar plunged in value on foreign currency markets.

If the economic problems weren't enough to make most everyone gloomy, the US political system hit an all-time low during this period as well. Vice President Spiro Agnew resigned in disgrace under a cloud of tax-evasion charges. Then Watergate led to President Richard Nixon's August 1974 resignation, the first presidential resignation in the nation's history.

_____

_____

_____

When all was sold and done, the Dow Jones Industrial Average plummeted more than 45 percent from early 1973 until late 1974. Among the stocks that fell the hardest were those that were most popular and selling at extreme multiples of earnings in the late 1960s and early 1970s.

Table 6-1 shows the drops in some well-known companies and how cheaply these stocks were valued relative to corporate profits (look at the P/E ratios) after the worst market drop since the Great Depression.

Those who were too terrified to buy stocks in the mid-1970s had time to get on board and take advantage of the buying opportunities. The stock market did have a powerful rally and, from its 1974 low, rose nearly 80 percent over the next two years. But over the next half dozen years, the market backpedaled, losing much of its gains.

During the 2008 financial crisis, panic (and talk of another Great Depression) was in the air and stock prices dropped sharply. Peak to trough, global stock prices plunged 50-plus percent. While some companies went under (and garnered lots of news headlines), those firms were few in number and were the exception rather than the norm. Many terrific companies weathered the storm, and their stock could be scooped up by investors with cash and courage at attractive prices and valuations.

Company	Industry	Stock Price Fall from Peak	1974 P/E
Abbott Laboratories	Drugs	66%	8
H&R Block	Tax preparation	83%	6
Chemical Bank	Banking	64%	4
Coca-Cola	Beverages	70%	12
Disney	Entertainment	75%	11
Dun & Bradstreet	Business information	68%	9
General Dynamics	Military	81%	3
Hilton Hotels	Hotels	87%	4
Humana	Hospitals	91%	3
Intel	Semiconductors	76%	6
Kimberly-Clark	Consumer products	63%	4
McGraw-Hill	Publishing	90%	4
Mobil	Oil	60%	3
PepsiCo	Beverages	67%	8
Pitney Bowes	Postage meters	84%	6
Quaker Oats	Packaged food	76%	6
Rite Aid	Drug stores	95%	4
Sprint	Telephone	67%	7

Table 6-1: *Stock Bargains in the Mid-1970s*

When bad news and pessimism abound and the stock market has dropped, it's actually a much safer and better time to buy stocks. You may even consider shifting some of your money out of your safer investments, such as bonds, and invest more aggressively in stocks. Investors feel during these times that prices can drop further, but if you buy and hold for the long term, you'll be amply rewarded. Most of the stocks listed in the preceding several pages have appreciated 500 to 2,500-plus percent in the subsequent decades.

Preparing to Invest in Stocks

There's always a chorus of self-anointed gurus saying you can make fat profits if you pick your own stocks. However, unless you're extraordinarily lucky or unusually gifted at analyzing company and investor behavior, you won't earn above-average returns if you select your own stocks.

Keep the amount that you dedicate to individual stock investments to a minimum — ideally, no more than 20 percent of your invested dollars. I encourage you to do such investing for the educational value and enjoyment that you derive from it, not because you smugly think you're as skilled as the best professional money managers.

Understanding stock prices

Just about every major financial and news site on the Internet offers stock quotes for free as a lure to get you to visit the site. To view a stock price quote online, all you need is the security's trading symbol (which you obtain by using the stock symbol look-up feature universally offered with online quote services). Most major newspapers print a listing of the prior day's stock prices. Daily business papers, such as *The Wall Street Journal* and *Investor's Business Daily*, also publish stock prices daily.

Cable business channels, such as Bloomberg, CNBC, and Fox Business, have stock quotes streaming across the bottom of the screen. You can stop by a local brokerage office and see the current stock quotes whizzing by on a long, narrow screen on a wall.

The following table is a typical example of the kinds of information that you can find in daily price quotes in papers and online; the quotes in this table are for the information technology giant International Business Machines (IBM). After the name of the company, you see the trading symbol, IBM, which is the code that you and brokers use to look up the price on computer-based quotation systems.

International Business Machines (IBM)	
52-wk range	172.19–211.98
Last trade	4:00 pm EST (196.47)
Change	+1.36 (+0.70%)
Day's range	194.35–196.86
Open	194.38
Volume	4,211,284
P/E ratio	13.4
Mkt cap	198.4B
Div/Shr	3.80
Yield	2.00%

Here's a breakdown of what the information in this table means:

- **52-week range:** These two numbers indicate the low ($172.19) and high ($211.98) trading prices for IBM during the past 52 weeks.
- **Last trade:** This line indicates the most recent price that the stock traded at (you can see that this IBM quote was

from 4:00 p.m. Eastern Standard Time, which is when the New York Stock Exchange closes for the day).

- **Change:** This entry indicates how that price differs from the previous day's close. In this case, you can see that the stock was up 1.36 points (0.70 percent) from the prior day's close.

- **Day's range:** These two numbers are the lowest and highest prices that the stock traded at during the day.

- **Open:** This line tells you the trade price at the market's open.

- **Volume:** This number indicates the number of shares that traded through this point in the trading day. (To conserve space, many newspapers indicate the volume in hundreds of shares — in other words, you must add two zeros to the end of the number to arrive at the actual number of shares.)

- **The P/E ratio:** As explained earlier in this chapter, the P/E ratio measures the price of IBM's stock relative to the company's earnings or profits.

- **Market capitalization (mkt cap):** This number tells you the current market value of all of IBM's stock, which in this case is $198.4 billion. You calculate this value by multiplying the current price per share by the total number of shares outstanding. (See Chapter 10 for an explanation of so-called market caps as they apply to stocks and stock funds.)

- **Dividends/share (div/shr):** This number shows you the current dividend (in this case, $3.80 per share), which the company pays yearly to shareholders. Most companies actually pay out one-quarter of their total annual dividend every three months.

- **Yield:** This number indicates the effective percentage yield that the stock's dividend produces. To calculate the effective yield, divide the dividend by the current stock price. Thus, IBM shareholders can expect to receive a dividend worth about 2.0 percent of the current stock price.

Purchasing stock "direct" from companies

Numerous companies sell their stock directly to the public. Proponents of these direct stock purchase plans say you can invest in stocks without paying any commissions. Well, the commission-free spiel isn't quite true, and investing in such plans poses other challenges.

_____

_____

_____

If you want to purchase directly from Home Depot, for example, you need a minimum initial investment of $500. Buying stock "direct" isn't free; in the case of Home Depot, for example, you have to pay a $5 enrollment fee. Although that may not sound like much on a $500 investment, $5 represents 1 percent of your investment. For subsequent purchases, you pay 5 percent up to a maximum of $2.50 per purchase plus 5 cents per share.

If you want to sell your shares, you have to pay a fee to do that, too — $25 plus 15 cents per share. Overall, these fees compare to what you would pay to buy stock through a discount broker (see Chapter 11 for details). In some cases, these fees are actually higher. For example, you can reinvest dividends at no cost through many discount brokers.

Some direct stock purchase plans entail even more hassle and cost than the type I just discussed. With other plans, you must buy your initial shares through a broker and then transfer your shares to the issuing company in order to buy more. Also, you can't pursue most direct stock purchase plans within retirement accounts.

Every time you want to set up a stock purchase plan with a company, you must request and complete the company's application forms. If you go through the headache of doing so, say, a dozen times, you're rewarded with a dozen statements on a regular basis from each individual company. Frankly, because of this drawback alone, I prefer to buy stock through a discount brokerage account that allows centralized purchasing and holding of various stocks as well as consolidated tax-reporting statements.

Placing your trade through a broker

Unless you decide to buy stock directly, you generally need a broker. As I explain in Chapter 11, discount brokers are the best way to go — they take your orders and charge far less than conventional brokerage firms, which generally pay their brokers on commission.

After you decide which discount broker you want to use, request (by phone or via the Internet) an account application package for the type of account you desire (non-retirement, IRA, and so on). Complete the forms (call the firm's toll-free number or visit a branch office if you get stuck) and return them to the discounter.

When you're ready to place your order, simply call the discount broker and explain what you want to do (or use your touch-tone phone or computer to place your order). You have two options:

- **Market order:** I recommend placing what's known as a *market order.* Such an order instructs your broker to buy the amount of stock that you desire (100 shares, for example) at the current and best (lowest) price available. With securities in which there's little trading or generally volatile price movements, market orders are a bit riskier. As a result, you may want to instead consider a limit order.

- **Limit order:** Alternatively, you can try to buy a desired stock at a specific price. For example, you can place a purchase order at $32.50 per share when the stock's last trade was $33 per share. This type of order is known as a *limit order* and is good until you cancel it. I don't recommend that you try this tactic, because it requires you to hope and gamble that the stock drops a little before it rises. If the stock simply rises from its current price of $33 per share or drops to $32.55 before it makes a big move higher, you may kick yourself. If you think the stock is a good buy for the long haul, buy it with a market order. If you don't think it's a good buy, don't buy it.

One final word of advice: Try to buy stock in good-size chunks, such as 100 shares. Otherwise, commissions gobble a large percentage of the small dollar amount that you invest. If you don't have enough money to build a diversified portfolio all at once, don't sweat it. Diversify over time. Purchase a chunk of one stock after you have enough money accumulated and then wait to buy the next stock until you've saved another chunk to invest.

7

Bonds and Bank Products

Lending investments are those in which you lend your money to an organization, such as a bank, company, or government, which typically pays you a fixed rate of interest. *Ownership investments*, by contrast, provide partial ownership of a company or some other asset, such as real estate, that has the ability to generate revenue and potential profits.

Lending investments aren't the best choice if you really want to make your money grow. However, even the most aggressive investors should consider placing some of their money into lending investments. The following table shows when such investments do and don't make sense.

Consider Lending Investments If...	Consider Ownership Investments When...
You need current income.	You don't need or want much current income.
You expect to sell within five years.	You're investing for the long term (seven to ten-plus years).
Investment volatility makes you a wreck, or you just want to cushion some of the volatility of your other riskier investments.	You don't mind or can ignore significant ups and downs.
You don't need to make your money grow after inflation and taxes.	You need more growth to reach your goals.

Lending investments are everywhere — banks, credit unions, brokerage firms, insurance companies, and mutual fund companies. Lending investments that you may have heard of include bank accounts (savings and certificates of deposit), Treasury bills and other bonds, bond mutual funds and exchange-traded bond funds, mortgages, and guaranteed-investment contracts.

In this chapter, I walk you through these investments, explain what's good and bad about each, and discuss situations in which you could consider using (or not using) them.

Bank Products

Putting your money in a bank may make you feel safe for a variety of reasons. If you're like most people, your first investing experience was at your neighborhood bank, where you established checking and savings accounts.

Part of the comfort of keeping money in the bank stems from the fact that the bank is where your parents may have first steered you financially. Also, at a local branch, often near your home or office, you find vaults, security-monitoring cameras, and barriers in front of the tellers. Most of these things shouldn't make you feel safer about leaving your money with the bank, however — they're needed because of bank robberies!

Bank branches cost a lot of money to operate. Guess where that money comes from. From bank depositors, of course! These operating costs are one of the reasons the interest rates that banks pay often pale in comparison to some of the similarly secure alternatives I discuss in this chapter.

Bank insurance

Some people are consoled by the Federal Deposit Insurance Corporation (FDIC) insurance that comes with bank accounts. It's true that if your bank fails, your account is insured by the US government up to $250,000. So what? Every Treasury bond is issued and backed by the federal government — the same organization that stands behind the FDIC. Plenty of other equally safe lending investments yield higher returns than bank accounts.

Just because the federal government stands behind the banking FDIC system doesn't mean your money is 100 percent safe in the event of a bank failure. Although you're insured for $250,000 in a bank, if the bank crashes, you may wait quite a while to get your money back — and you may get less interest than you thought you would. Banks fail and will continue to fail. During the 1980s and early 1990s, and again in the late 2000s, hundreds of insured banks and savings and loans failed annually. (Between the early 1990s and late 2000s, only a handful of banks failed annually.)

Any investment that involves lending your money to someone else or to some organization, including putting your money in a bank or buying a Treasury bond that the federal government issues, carries risk.

_____

_____

_____

Online banking

With the continued growth of the online world, you can find more and more banking options online. Of particular appeal are higher-interest online savings accounts. The best of them do pay higher interest rates than their brick-and-mortar peers and money market funds.

Online banks don't generally have any or many retail branches; they conduct most of their business over the Internet and through the mail. By lowering the costs of doing business, the best online banks may offer better account terms, such as paying you higher interest rates on your account balances. Online banks can also offer better terms on loans.

Online banking is convenient, too. It's generally available 24/7. You can usually conduct most transactions more quickly on the Internet, and by banking online, you save the bank money, which enables the bank to offer you better deals.

Here's the issue I have with online banks: With many online accounts, you face fees and hassles to actually access your money. Also, if you're looking to park a major chunk of money for a long time, you can do better, for example, with safe bond funds.

Technology allows you to do more and more banking online. But remember to protect yourself and your money. You need to put on your detective hat when investigating online banks and be ready to do some searching for the best and safest deals. Never pick a bank simply because you saw one of its ads or because you know a co-worker who uses that bank. These sections tell you what you need to do to evaluate an online bank and how to make the most of banking online.

FDIC coverage

So what do you look for in an online bank? First you need to select a bank that participates in the US government-operated Federal Deposit Insurance Corporation (FDIC) program. Otherwise, if the online bank you choose fails, your money isn't protected. The FDIC covers your deposits at each bank up to $250,000.

To see whether a bank is covered, never simply take the bank's word for it or accept the bank's display of the FDIC logo on its website or in its offices as proof. Instead, go to the FDIC's BankFind page (http://research.fdic.gov/bankfind) to search the database of FDIC-insured institutions. You can search by the bank's name, city, state, or zip code. For an insured bank, you can see the date it became insured, its insurance certificate number, the main office location for the bank (and branches), its primary government regulator, and other links to detailed information about the bank. In the event that your bank doesn't appear on the FDIC list yet claims FDIC coverage, contact the FDIC at 877-275-3342.

Beware that some online banks are able to offer higher interest rates because they're based overseas and don't participate in the FDIC program. Participating banks in the FDIC program must pay insurance premiums into the FDIC fund, which, of course, adds to a bank's costs.

Other online bank issues

In addition to ensuring that a bank is covered by the FDIC, you should get answers to the following questions:

- **What's the bank's reputation for its services?**
  Reputation isn't an easy thing to investigate, but at a minimum, you can conduct an Internet search of the bank's name along with the word "complaints" or "problems" and examine the results.

_____

_____

_____

- **How accessible and knowledgeable are the customer service people?** You want to be able to speak with a helpful person when you need assistance. Look for a phone number on the online bank's website and call it to see how much trouble you have reaching a live person. Ask the customer service representatives questions (including the following) to determine how knowledgeable and service oriented they are.

- **What are the processes and options for withdrawing your money?** This issue is important to discuss with the bank's customer service people because you want convenient, low-cost access to your money. For example, if a bank lacks ATMs, what does the bank charge you for using other ATMs?

- **What are the fees for particular services?** You can typically find this information on the bank's website in a section titled "Account Terms" or "Disclosures." Also, look for the "Truth in Savings Disclosure," which answers relevant account questions in a standardized format.

Certificates of deposit (CDs)

Other than savings accounts, banks also sell *certificates of deposit* (CDs). CDs are an often overused bank investment — investors use them by default, often without researching their pros and cons. The attraction is that you may get a higher rate of return on a CD than on a bank savings or money market account. And unlike a bond (which I discuss in the "Why Bother with Bonds?" section later in this chapter), a CD's principal value doesn't fluctuate. CDs also give you the peace of mind afforded by the government's FDIC insurance program.

The reason that CDs pay higher interest rates than savings accounts is that you commit to tie up your money for a period of time, such as 6, 12, or 24 months. The bank pays you 1 to 2 percent and then turns around and lends your money to others through credit cards, auto loans, real estate loans, business loans, and so on. The bank then charges those borrowers an interest rate of 6, 8, 10 percent, or more. Not a bad business!

When you tie up your money in a CD and later decide you want it back before the CD matures, a hefty penalty (typically about six months' interest) is shaved from your return. With other lending investments, such as bonds and bond mutual funds, you can access your money without penalty and generally at little or no cost.

In addition to penalties for early withdrawal, CDs yield less than a high-quality bond with a comparable maturity (for example, two, five, or ten years). Often, the yield difference is 1 percent or more, especially if you don't shop around and simply buy CDs from the local bank where you keep your checking account.

High-tax-bracket investors who purchase CDs outside of their retirement accounts should be aware of a final and perhaps fatal flaw of CDs: The interest on CDs is fully taxable at the federal and state levels. Bonds, by contrast, are available (if you desire) in tax-free (federal and/or state) versions.

You can earn higher returns and have better access to your money when it's in high-quality bonds than you can when it's in CDs. Bonds make especially good sense when you're in a higher tax bracket and would benefit from tax-free income in a non-retirement account. CDs make the most sense when you know, for example, that you can invest your money for one year, after which you need the money for some purchase that you expect to make. Just make sure you shop around to get the best interest rate. If having the US government insurance gives you peace of mind, also take a look at Treasury bonds, which

I discuss later in this chapter. Treasury bonds (also known as *Treasuries*) tend to pay more interest than many CDs.

Money market funds

Because bank accounts generally pay pretty crummy interest rates, you need to think long and hard about keeping your spare cash in the bank. You can, if you so choose, keep your checking account at your local bank. But you don't have to.

Instead of relying on the bank as a place to keep your extra savings, try *money market funds,* which are a type of mutual fund that doesn't focus on bonds or stocks. Money market funds offer a higher-yielding alternative to bank savings and bank money market deposit accounts.

Money market funds, which are offered by mutual fund companies (see Chapter 9), are unique among mutual funds because they don't fluctuate in value and because they maintain a fixed $1-per-share price. As with a bank savings account, your principal investment in a money market fund doesn't change in value. If you invest your money in a money market fund, it earns *dividends* (which are just another name for the interest you'd receive in a bank account).

Money market fund advantages

The best money market mutual funds offer the following benefits over traditional bank savings accounts:

- **They provide higher yields.** The best money market mutual funds historically have paid higher yields because they don't have the high overhead that banks do. The most efficient mutual fund companies don't have scads of branch offices. (Here's an exception to the higher-yields rule: The extended period of ultra-low interest rates following the severe recession of 2008 took away the yield advantage of money market funds.)

  Banks can get away with paying lower yields because they know that many depositors believe that the FDIC insurance that comes with a bank savings account makes it safer than a money market mutual fund. Also, the FDIC insurance is an expense that banks ultimately pass on to their customers.

- **They come in a variety of tax-free versions.** If you're in a high tax bracket (see Chapter 3), tax-free money market funds offer you something that bank accounts don't.

Another useful feature of money market mutual funds is the ability they provide you to write checks, without charge, against your account. Most mutual fund companies require that the checks you write be for larger amounts — typically at least $250. They don't want you using these accounts to pay all your small household bills because checks cost money to process.

However, a few money market funds (such as those that brokerage cash management accounts at firms like Charles Schwab, TD Ameritrade, Vanguard, and Fidelity) allow you to write checks for any amount and can completely replace a bank checking account. Do keep in mind that some brokerage firms hit you with service fees if you don't have enough assets with them or don't have regular monthly electronic transfers, such as through direct deposit of your paycheck or money transfer from your bank account. With these types of money market funds, you can leave your bank altogether because these brokerage accounts often come with debit cards that you can use at bank ATMs for a nominal fee.

Money market funds are a good place to keep your emergency cash reserve of at least three to six months' living expenses. They're also a great place to keep money awaiting investment elsewhere in the near future. If you're saving money for a home that you expect to purchase soon (in the next year or so), a money market fund can be a safe place to accumulate and grow the down payment. You don't want to risk placing such money in the stock market because the market can plunge in a relatively short period of time.

Just as you can use a money market fund for your personal purposes, you also can open a money market fund for your business. You can use this account to deposit checks that you receive from customers, to hold excess funds, and to pay bills via the check-writing feature.

Money market fund disadvantages

Higher yields, tax-free alternatives, and check writing — money market funds almost sound too good to be true. What's the catch? Good money market funds really don't have a catch, but you need to know about one difference between bank accounts and money market mutual funds: Money market funds aren't insured (however, they were for a one-year period during the 2008–2009 financial crisis).

As I discuss earlier in this chapter, bank accounts come with FDIC insurance that protects your deposited money up to $250,000. So if a bank fails because it lends too much money to people and companies that go bankrupt or abscond with the funds, you should get your money back from the FDIC.

The lack of FDIC insurance on a money market fund shouldn't trouble you. Mutual fund companies can't fail, because they have a dollar invested in securities for every dollar you deposit in their money market funds. By contrast, banks are required to have available just a portion, such as 10 to 12 cents, for every dollar you hand over to them (the exact amount depends on the type of deposit).

A money market fund's investments can decline slightly in value, which can cause the money market fund's share price to fall below a dollar. Cases have occurred where money market funds bought some bad investments (this happened more during the 2008–2009 financial crisis). However, in nearly every case, the parent company running the money market fund infused cash into the affected fund, thus enabling it to maintain the $1-per-share price.

The only money market funds that did "break the buck" didn't take in money from people like you or me; in one case, the fund was run by a bunch of small banks for themselves. This money market fund made some poor investments. The share price of the fund declined by 6 percent, and the fund owners decided to disband the fund; they didn't bail it out because they would have been repaying themselves. In another case, a money market fund that took in money from institutions declined by 3 percent.

 Stick with bigger mutual fund companies if you're worried about the lack of FDIC insurance (or consider an online bank savings account with FDIC and reasonable fees). These companies have the financial wherewithal and the largest incentive to save a foundering money market fund. Fortunately, the bigger fund companies have the best money market funds anyway. You can find more details about money market funds in Chapter 9.

Why Bother with Bonds?

Conservative investors prefer bonds (that is, conservative when it comes to taking risk, not when professing their political orientation). Otherwise-aggressive investors who seek diversification or investments for shorter-term financial goals also prefer bonds. The reason? Bonds offer higher yields than bank accounts, usually without the volatility of the stock market.

Bonds are similar to CDs, except that bonds are securities that trade in the market with a fluctuating value. For example, you can purchase a bond, scheduled to mature five years from now, that a company such as Wal-Mart issues. A Wal-Mart five-year bond may pay you 5.25 percent interest. The company sends you interest payments on the bond for five years. And as long as Wal-Mart doesn't have a financial catastrophe, the company returns your original investment to you after the five years is up. So in effect, you're lending your money to Wal-Mart (instead of to the bank when you deposit money in a bank account).

The worst that can happen to your bond investment is that the business goes into a tailspin and the company ends up in financial ruin — also known as bankruptcy. If the company does go bankrupt, you may lose all your original investment and miss out on the remaining interest payments you were supposed to receive.

But bonds that high-quality companies issue are quite safe — they rarely default. Besides, you don't have to invest all your money earmarked for bonds in just one or two bonds. If you own bonds in many companies (which you can easily do through a bond mutual fund or exchange-traded fund) and one bond unexpectedly takes a hit, it affects only a small portion of your portfolio. And unlike CDs, you can generally sell your bonds anytime you want at minimal cost. (Selling and buying most bond mutual funds costs nothing, as I explain in Chapter 8.)

Bond investors accept the risk of default because bonds generally pay you more than bank savings accounts and money market mutual funds. But there's a catch. As I discuss in Chapter 8, bonds are riskier than money market funds and savings accounts because their value can fall if interest rates rise. Plus you're forgoing the security of FDIC insurance (which bank accounts have). However, bonds tend to be more stable in value than stocks. (I cover the risks and returns of bonds and stocks in Chapter 2.)

Investing in bonds is a time-honored way to earn a better rate of return on money you don't plan to use within the next couple of years or more. As with stocks, bonds can generally be sold any day that the financial markets are open. Because their value fluctuates, though, you're more likely to lose money if you're forced to sell your bonds sooner rather than later. In the short term, if the bond market happens to fall and you need to sell, you could lose money. In the longer term, as is the case with stocks, you're far less likely to lose money.

Don't put your emergency cash reserve into bonds — that's what a money market fund or bank savings account is for. And don't put too much of your longer-term investment money into bonds, either. As I explain in Chapter 2, bonds are generally inferior investments for making your money grow. Growth-oriented investments, such as stocks, real estate, and your own business, hold the greatest potential to build wealth.

Here are some common situations in which investing in bonds can make sense:

- **You're looking to make a major purchase.** This purchase should be one that won't happen for at least two years, such as buying a home or some other major expenditure. Shorter-term bonds may work for you as a higher-yielding and slightly riskier alternative to money market funds.

- **You want to diversify your portfolio.** Bonds don't move in tandem with the performance of other types of investments, such as stocks. In fact, in a terrible economic environment (such as during the Great Depression in the early 1930s or the financial crisis of 2008), bonds may appreciate in value while riskier investments such as stocks plunge.

- **You're interested in long-term investments.** You may invest some of your money in bonds as part of a longer-term investment strategy, such as for retirement. You should have an overall plan for how you want to invest your money, sometimes referred to as an *asset allocation strategy* (see Chapter 9). Aggressive, younger investors should keep less of their retirement money in bonds than older folks who are nearing retirement.

- **You need income-producing investments.** If you're retired or not working much, bonds can be useful because they're better at producing current income than many other investments.

Different Types of Bonds

Bonds differ from one another according to a number of factors — length (number of years) to maturity, credit quality, and the entities that issue the bonds (the latter of which has tax implications that you need to be aware of). After you have a handle on these issues, you're ready to consider investing in individual bonds and bond mutual funds and exchange-traded funds.

Unfortunately, due to shady marketing practices by some investing companies and salespeople who sell bonds, you can have your work cut out for you while trying to get a handle on what many bonds really are and how they differ from their peers. In the following sections, I help you make sense of the different types of bonds.

Maturity

Maturity simply means the time at which the bond promises to pay back your principal — next year, in 7 years, in 15 years, and so on. A bond's maturity gives you a good (although far-from-perfect) sense of how volatile a bond may be if interest rates change. If interest rates fall, bond prices rise; if interest rates rise, bond prices fall. Longer-term bonds drop more in price when the overall level of interest rates rises.

Suppose you're considering investing in two bonds that the same organization issues, and both yield 7 percent. The bonds differ from one another only in when they'll mature: One is a 2-year bond; the other is a 20-year bond. If interest rates were to rise just 1 percent (from 7 percent to 8 percent), the 2-year bond may decline about 2 percent in value, whereas the 20-year bond could fall approximately five times as much — 10 percent.

If you hold a bond until it matures, you get your principal back, unless the issuer defaults. In the meantime, however, if interest rates rise, bond prices fall. The reason is simple: If the bond that you hold is issued at, say, 7 percent, and interest rates on similar bonds rise to 8 percent, no one wants to purchase your 7 percent bond. The value of your bond has to decrease enough so it effectively yields 8 percent.

Bonds are generally classified by the length of time until maturity:

- Short-term bonds mature in the next few years.
- Intermediate-term bonds come due within 3 to 10 years.
- Long-term bonds mature in more than 10 years, generally up to 30 years.

Most of the time, longer-term bonds pay higher yields than short-term bonds. You can look at a chart of the current yield of similar bonds plotted against when they mature — such a chart is known as a *yield curve*. Most of the time, this curve slopes upward. Investors generally demand a higher rate of interest for taking the risk of holding longer-term bonds.

Likelihood of default

In addition to being issued for various lengths of time, bonds differ from one another in the creditworthiness of the issuer. To minimize investing in bonds that default, purchase highly rated bonds. Credit-rating agencies such as Moody's, Standard & Poor's, and Fitch rate the credit quality and likelihood of default of bonds.

The *credit rating* of a bond depends on the issuer's ability to pay back its debt. Bond credit ratings are usually done on some sort of a letter-grade scale where, for example, AAA is the highest rating and ratings descend through AA and A, followed by BBB, BB, B, CCC, CC, C, and so on. Here's the lowdown on the ratings:

- **AAA- and AA-rated bonds** are considered *high-grade* or *high-credit quality bonds*. Such bonds possess little chance — a fraction of 1 percent — of default.

- **A- and BBB-rated bonds** are considered *investment-grade* or *general-quality bonds*.

- **BB- or lower-rated bonds** are known as *junk bonds* (or by their marketed name, *high-yield bonds*). Junk bonds, also known as *non-investment grade bonds*, are more likely to default — perhaps as many as a couple of percent per year actually default.

Why would any sane investor buy a bond with a low credit rating? He may purchase one of these bonds because issuers pay a higher interest rate on lower-quality bonds to attract investors. The lower a bond's credit rating and quality, the higher the yield you can and should expect from such a bond. Poorer-quality bonds, though, aren't for the faint of heart because they're generally more volatile in value.

I don't recommend buying individual junk bonds — consider investing in these only through a well-run junk-bond fund.

Bond issuers (and tax implications)

Besides varying in credit ratings and maturity, bonds also differ from one another according to the type of organization that issues them — in other words, what kind of organization you lend your money to. The following sections go over the most common options and tell you when each option may make sense for you.

Treasury bonds

Treasuries are IOUs from the US government. The types of Treasury bonds include Treasury *bills* (which mature within a year), Treasury *notes* (which mature between one and ten years), and Treasury *bonds* (which mature in more than ten years). These distinctions and delineations are arbitrary — you don't need to know them.

Treasuries pay interest that's state-tax-free but federally taxable. Thus, they make sense if you want to avoid a high state-income-tax bracket but not a high federal-income-tax bracket. However, most people in a high state-income-tax bracket also happen to be in a high federal-income-tax bracket. Such high-tax-bracket investors may be better off in municipal bonds (explained in the next section), which are both federal- and state-income-tax-free (in their state of issuance).

The best use of Treasuries is in place of bank CDs. If you feel secure with the federal government insurance (which is limited to $250,000) that a bank CD provides, check out a Treasury bond (which has the unlimited backing of the US government). Treasuries that mature in the same length of time as a CD may pay the same or a better interest rate. Remember that bank CD interest is fully taxable, whereas a Treasury's interest is state-tax-free. Unless you really shop for a bank CD, you'll likely earn a lower return on a CD than on a Treasury. I explain how to purchase Treasury bonds in Chapter 8.

Municipal bonds

Municipal bonds are state and local government bonds that pay interest that's federal-tax-free and state-tax-free to residents in the state of issue. For example, if you live in California and buy a bond issued by a California government agency, you probably won't owe California state or federal income tax on the interest.

The government organizations that issue municipal bonds know that the investors who buy these bonds don't have to pay most or any of the income tax that's normally required on other bonds — which means that the issuing governments can pay a lower rate of interest.

If you're in a high tax bracket and want to invest in bonds outside of your tax-sheltered retirement accounts, you may end up with a higher after-tax yield from a municipal bond (often called *muni*) than from a comparable bond that pays taxable interest. Compare the yield on a given municipal bond (or muni bond fund) to the after-tax yield on a comparable taxable bond (or bond fund).

Corporate bonds

Companies such as Boeing and Johnson & Johnson issue corporate bonds. *Corporate bonds* pay interest that's fully taxable. Thus, they're appropriate for investing inside retirement accounts. Lower-tax-bracket investors should consider buying such bonds outside a tax-sheltered retirement account. (Higher-bracket investors should instead consider municipal bonds, which I discuss in the preceding section.) In Chapter 8, I show you how to read price listings for such bonds.

8

Purchasing Bonds

You can invest in bonds in one of two major ways: You can purchase individual bonds, or you can invest in a professionally selected and managed portfolio of bonds via a bond mutual fund or exchange-traded fund (see Chapters 9 and 10).

In this chapter, I help you decide how to invest in bonds. If you want to take the individual-bond route, I cover that path here, where I explain how to decipher bond listings you find in financial newspapers or online. I also explain the purchasing process for Treasuries (a different animal in that you can buy them directly from the government) and all other bonds. If you fall on the side of funds, head to Chapters 9 and 10 for more information.

Individual Bonds versus Bond Funds

Unless the bonds you're considering purchasing are easy to analyze and homogeneous (such as Treasury bonds), you're generally better off investing in bonds through a mutual fund or exchange-traded fund. Here's why:

- **Diversification is more difficult with individual bonds.** You shouldn't put your money into a small number of bonds of companies in the same industry or that mature at the same time. It's difficult to cost-effectively build a diversified bond portfolio with individual issues, unless you have a substantial amount of money ($1 million) that you want to invest in bonds.

- **Individual bonds cost you more money.** If you purchase individual bonds through a broker, you're going to pay a commission. In most cases, the commission cost is hidden — the broker quotes you a price for the bond that includes the commission. Even if you use a discount broker, these fees take a healthy bite out of your investment. The smaller the amount you invest, the bigger the bite — on a $1,000 bond, the commission fee can equal several percent. Commissions take a smaller bite out of larger bonds — perhaps less than 0.5 percent if you use discount brokers.

On the other hand, investing in bonds through a fund is cost-effective. Great bond funds are yours for less than 0.5 percent per year in operating expenses. Selecting good bond funds isn't hard, as I explain in Chapter 10.

- **You have better things to do with your time.** Do you really want to research bonds and go bond shopping? Bonds are boring to most people! And bonds and the companies that stand behind them aren't that simple to understand. For example, did you know that some bonds can be called before their maturity dates? Companies often *call* bonds (which means they repay the principal before maturity) to save money if interest rates drop significantly. After you purchase a bond, you need to do the same things that a good bond mutual fund portfolio manager needs to do, such as track the issuer's creditworthiness and monitor other important financial developments.

Bond Prices

Business-focused publications and websites provide daily bond pricing. You may also call a broker or browse websites to obtain bond prices. The following steps walk you through the bond listing for PhilEl (Philadelphia Electric) in Figure 8-1:

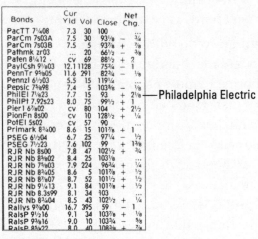

Figure 8-1: *Sample bond listings.*

- **Bond name:** This column tells you who issued the bond. In this case, the issuer is a large utility company, Philadelphia Electric.

- **Funny numbers after the company name:** The first part of the numerical sequence here — 7 1/8 — refers to the original interest rate (7.125 percent) that this bond paid when it was issued. This interest rate is known as the *coupon rate*, which is a percent of the maturity value of the bond. The second part of the numbers — 23 — refers to the year that the bond matures (2023, in this case).

- **Current yield:** Divide the interest paid, 7.125, by the current price per bond, $93, to arrive at the current yield. In this case, it equals (rounded off) 7.7 percent.

- **Volume:** Volume indicates the number of bonds that traded on this day. In the case of PhilEl, 15 bonds were traded.

- **Close:** This shows the last price at which the bond traded. The last PhilEl bond price is $93.

- **Change:** The change indicates how this day's close compares with the previous day's close. In the example figure, the bond rose 2 1/8 points. Some bonds don't trade all that often. Notice that some bonds were up and others were down on this particular day. The demand of new buyers and the supply of interested sellers influence the price movement of a given bond.

In addition to the direction of overall interest rates, changes in the financial health of the issuing entity that stands behind the bond strongly affect the price of an individual bond.

Purchasing Treasuries

If you want to purchase Treasury bonds, buying them through the Treasury Direct program is the lowest-cost option. Call 800-722-2678 or visit the US Department of Treasury's website (www.treasurydirect.gov).

You may also purchase and hold Treasury bonds through brokerage firms and mutual funds. Brokers typically charge a flat fee for buying a Treasury bond. Buying Treasuries through a brokerage account makes sense if you hold other securities through the brokerage account and you like the ability to quickly sell a Treasury bond. Selling Treasury bonds held through Treasury Direct requires you to transfer the bonds to a broker.

The advantage of a fund that invests in Treasuries is that it typically holds Treasuries of differing maturities, thus offering diversification. You can generally buy and sell *no-load* (commission-free) Treasury bond mutual funds easily and without fees. Funds, however, do charge an ongoing management fee.

Purchasing Other Individual Bonds

Purchasing other types of individual bonds, such as corporate and mortgage bonds, is a much more treacherous and time-consuming undertaking than buying Treasuries. Here's my advice for doing it right and minimizing the chance of mistakes:

- **Don't buy through salespeople.** Brokerage firms that employ representatives on commission are in the sales business. Many of the worst bond-investing disasters have befallen customers of such brokerage firms. Your best bet is to purchase individual bonds through discount brokers (see Chapter 11).

- **Don't be suckered into high yields — buy quality.**
Yes, junk bonds pay higher yields, but they also have a
much higher chance of default. Stick with highly rated
bonds so you don't have to worry about and suffer
through these consequences.

- **Understand that bonds may be called early.** Many
bonds, especially corporate bonds, can legally be called
before maturity. In this case, the bond issuer pays
you back early because it doesn't need to borrow as
much money or because interest rates have fallen and
the borrower wants to reissue new bonds at a lower
interest rate. Be especially careful about purchasing
bonds that were issued at higher interest rates than
those that currently prevail. Borrowers pay off such
bonds first.

- **Diversify.** To buffer changes in the economy that
adversely affect one industry or a few industries more
than others, invest in and hold bonds from a variety
of companies in different industries. Of the money
that you want to invest in bonds, don't put more than
5 percent into any one bond; that means you need to
hold at least 20 bonds. Diversification requires a good

amount to invest, given the size of most bonds and because trading fees erode your investment balance if you invest too little. If you can't achieve this level of diversification, use a bond mutual fund or ETF.

- **Shop around.** Shop around for good prices on the bonds you have in mind. The hard part is doing an apples-to-apples comparison because different brokers may not offer the same exact bonds. Remember that the two biggest determinants of what a bond should yield are its maturity date and its credit rating (see Chapter 7).

Unless you invest in boring, simple-to-understand bonds such as Treasuries, you're better off investing in bonds via the best bond mutual funds. One exception is if you absolutely, positively must receive your principal back on a certain date. Because bond funds don't mature, individual bonds with the correct maturity for you may best suit your needs. Consider Treasuries because they carry such a low default risk. Otherwise, you need a lot of time, money, and patience to invest well in individual bonds.

9

Mutual Funds and Exchange-Traded Funds

Different types of mutual funds and exchange-traded funds can help you meet various financial goals, which is why investors have more than $15 trillion invested in these funds! You can use money market funds for something most everybody needs: an emergency savings stash of three to six months' living expenses. Or perhaps you're thinking about saving for a home purchase, retirement, or future educational costs. If so, you can consider some stock and bond funds. Because efficient funds take most of the hassle and cost out of deciding which companies to invest in, they're among the finest investment vehicles available today.

Distinguishing between Mutual Funds and Exchange-Traded Funds

Mutual funds are big pools of money from investors that a fund manager uses to buy a bunch of stocks, bonds, and other assets that meet the fund's investment criteria.

Exchange-traded funds (ETFs) are similar to mutual funds in that they also invest a pot of investors' money into stocks, bonds, and so on. The most significant difference is that in order to invest in an ETF, you must buy it through a stock exchange where ETFs trade, just as individual stocks trade. Thus, you need a brokerage account to invest in ETFs. (See Chapter 11 for information on selecting a brokerage firm.)

Most ETFs are also like index mutual funds (see Chapter 10) in that each ETF generally tracks a major market index. The best ETFs may also have slightly lower operating expenses than the lowest-cost index mutual funds. However, you must pay a brokerage fee to buy and sell an ETF, and the current market price of the ETF may deviate slightly from the underlying market value of the securities in its portfolio.

Regardless of whether you choose to invest in a mutual fund or an ETF, good funds enable you to have some of the best money managers in the country direct the investment of your money.

Benefits of Funds

The best funds are superior investment vehicles for people of all economic means, and they can help you accomplish many financial objectives. The following sections go over the main reasons for investing in funds rather than individual securities. (If you wish to invest in individual stocks, I provide information on how best to do so in Chapters 4 through 6.)

Professional management

The fund investment company hires a portfolio manager and researchers whose full-time jobs are to analyze and purchase suitable investments for the fund. These people screen the universe of investments for those that meet the fund's stated objectives.

Typically, fund managers are graduates of the top business and finance schools, where they learned portfolio management and securities valuation and selection. Many have additional investing credentials, such as being a Chartered Financial Analyst (CFA). In addition to their educational training, the best fund managers typically possess ten or more years of experience in analyzing and selecting investments.

For most fund managers and researchers, finding the best investments is more than a full-time job. A fund management team does more research, number crunching, and due diligence than most people could ever have the energy or expertise to do in what little free time they have. Investing in funds frees up time for friendships, family relationships, and your favorite activities — don't miss the terrific time-saving benefits of fund investing!

Cost efficiency

Mutual funds and exchange-traded funds offer a cheaper, more communal way of getting your investment work done. When you invest your money in an efficiently managed fund, it likely costs you less than trading individual securities on your own.

Fund managers can buy and sell securities for a fraction of the cost you pay.

Funds also spread the cost of research over thousands of investors. The most efficiently managed funds cost less than 1 percent per year in fees. Some of the larger and more established funds can charge annual fees of less than 0.2 percent per year — that's less than a $2 annual charge per $1,000 you invest.

Diversification

Diversification is a big attraction for many investors who choose funds. Most funds own stocks or bonds from dozens of companies, thus diversifying against the risk of bad news from any single company or sector. Achieving such diversification on your own is difficult and expensive unless you have a few hundred thousand dollars and a great deal of time to invest.

Funds typically invest in 25 to 100 securities or more. Proper diversification increases the fund's chances of earning higher returns with less risk.

Reasonable investment minimums

Most funds have low minimum investment requirements. Many funds have minimums of $1,000 or less. Retirement account investors can often invest with even less. Some funds even offer monthly investment plans so you can start with as little as $50 per month.

Different funds for different folks

Some people think that funds = stock market investing = risky. This line of thinking is wrong. The majority of money in funds isn't in the stock market. You can select the funds that take on the kinds of risks that you're comfortable with and that meet your financial goals. Following is a list of the three major types of funds:

- **Stock funds:** If you want your money to grow over a long period of time (and you can handle down as well as up years), choose funds that invest more heavily in stocks.

- **Bond funds:** If you need current income and don't want investments that fluctuate as widely in value as stocks do, consider some bond funds.

_____

_____

_____

- **Money market funds:** If you want to be sure that your invested principal doesn't decline in value because you may need to use your money in the short term, select a money market fund.

Most investors choose a combination of these three types of funds to diversify and help accomplish different financial goals. (I cover each type of fund in depth in Chapter 10.)

High financial safety

Thousands of banks and insurance companies have failed in recent decades. Banks and insurers can fail because their *liabilities* (the money that customers gave them to invest, which may need to be returned on short notice) can exceed their *assets* (the money that they've invested or lent).

For example, when big chunks of a bank's loans go sour at the same time that its depositors want their money, the bank fails; banks typically have less than 15 cents on deposit for every dollar that you and I place with them. Likewise, if an insurance company makes several poor investments or underestimates the number of insurance policyholder claims, it, too, can fail.

Such failures can't happen with a mutual fund or exchange-traded fund because the value of the fund's shares fluctuates as the securities in the fund rise and fall in value. For every dollar of securities they hold for their customers, funds have a dollar's worth of securities. The worst that can happen with a fund is that if you want your money, you may get less money than you originally put into the fund due to a market value decline of the fund's holdings — but you won't lose all your original investment.

Accessibility

What's really terrific about dealing with funds is that they're set up for people who value their time and don't like going to a local branch office and standing in long lines. With fund investing, you can fill out a simple form (often online) and write a check in the comfort of your home (or authorize electronic transfers from your bank or other accounts) to make your initial investment. You can then typically make subsequent investments by mailing in a check or sending in money electronically.

Selling shares of your funds is usually simple. Generally, all you need to do is call the fund company's toll-free number or visit its website. Some companies have representatives available around the clock, year-round. Most fund companies also offer online account access and trading capabilities as well.

Keys to Successful Fund Investing

This chapter helps explain why mutual and exchange-traded funds are good investment vehicles to use. However, keep in mind that not all funds are worthy of your investment dollars.

When you select a fund, you can use a number of simple, common-sense criteria to greatly increase your chances of investment success. The criteria presented in the following sections have been proven to dramatically increase your fund investing returns.

Minimize costs

The charges that you pay to buy or sell a fund, as well as the ongoing fund operating expenses, can have a big impact on the rate of return that you earn on your investments. Because hundreds of choices are available for a particular type of fund (larger-company US stock funds, for example), you have no reason to put up with inflated costs.

Fund costs are an important factor in the return that you earn from a fund because fees are deducted from your investment returns and can attack a fund from many angles. All other things being equal, high fees and other charges depress your returns.

 Stick with funds that maintain low total operating expenses and that don't charge *sales loads* (commissions). Both types of fees come out of your pocket and reduce your rate of return. Plenty of excellent funds are available at reasonable annual operating expense ratios (less than 1 percent for stock funds; less than 0.5 percent for bond funds).

Avoid load funds

The first fee you need to minimize is the *sales load*, which is a commission paid to brokers and financial planners who work on commission and sell mutual funds. Commissions, or *loads*, generally range from 4.0 to 8.5 percent of the amount you invest. Sales loads are an additional and unnecessary cost that's deducted from your investment money. You can find plenty of outstanding *no-load* (commission-free) funds.

Some mutual fund companies, such as Fidelity, try to play it both ways. They sell load funds (through brokers) as well as no-load funds (direct to investors). Be aware of this when a financial advisor says he can get you into funds from the leading companies, such as Fidelity, because what he really may be telling you is that he's pitching load funds.

Beware of high operating expenses

In addition to loads, the other costs of owning funds are the ongoing *operating expenses.* All funds charge fees as long as you keep your money in the fund. The fees pay for the costs of running a fund, such as employees' salaries, marketing, toll-free phone lines, designing and distributing *prospectuses* (legal disclosure of the fund's operations and fees), and so on.

A fund's operating expenses are essentially invisible to you because they're deducted from the fund's share price. Companies charge operating expenses on a daily basis, so you don't need to worry about trying to get out of a fund at a particular time of the year before the company deducts these fees.

All types of funds with higher operating expenses tend to produce lower rates of return on average. Conversely, funds with lower operating costs can more easily produce higher returns for you than a comparable type of fund with high costs. This effect makes sense because companies deduct operating expenses from the returns that your fund generates. Higher expenses mean a lower return to you.

Fund companies quote a fund's operating expenses as a percentage of your investment. The percentage represents an annual fee or charge. You can find this number in a fund's prospectus, in the fund expenses section, usually in a line that says something like "Total Fund Operating Expenses." You also can call the fund's toll-free phone number and ask a representative, or you can find the information at the fund company's website. Make sure a fund doesn't appear to have low expenses simply because it's temporarily waiving them. (You can ask the fund representative or look at the fees in the fund's prospectus to find this information.)

Reflect on performance and risk

A fund's historical rate of return or performance is another important factor to weigh when you select a fund. However, keep in mind that, as all fund materials must tell you, past performance is no guarantee of future results. In fact, many former high-return funds achieved their results only by taking on high risk or simply by relying on short-term luck. Funds that assume higher risk should produce higher rates of return. But high-risk funds usually decline in price faster during major market declines. Thus, a good fund should consistently deliver a favorable rate of return given the level of risk that it takes.

A big mistake that many investors make when they choose a fund is overemphasizing the importance of past performance numbers. Although past performance *can* be a good sign, high returns for a fund, relative to its peers, are largely possible only if a fund takes more risk.

Consider index funds

Index funds are funds that are mostly managed by a computer. Unlike other funds, in which the portfolio manager and a team of analysts scour the market for the best securities, an index fund manager simply invests to match the makeup, and thus also the performance, of an index (such as the Standard & Poor's 500 index of 500 large US company stocks). Most ETFs are simply index funds that trade on a stock exchange.

Index funds deliver relatively good returns by keeping expenses low, staying invested, and not trying to jump around.

Over ten years or more, index funds typically outperform about three-quarters of their peers. Most actively managed funds can't overcome the handicap of high operating expenses that pull down their rates of return. Index funds can run with far lower operating expenses because significant ongoing research isn't needed to identify companies to invest in.

The average US stock mutual fund, for example, has an operating expense ratio of 1.2 percent per year. (Some funds charge expenses as high as 2 percent or more per year.) That being the case, a US stock index fund with an expense ratio of just 0.2 percent per year has an advantage of 1.0 percent per year over the average fund. A 1.0 percent difference may not seem like much, but in fact it's a significant difference. Because stocks tend to return about 9 percent per year, you end up throwing away about 11 percent of your expected (pre-tax) stock fund returns with an "average fund" in terms of expenses (and an even greater portion of your post-tax returns).

With actively managed stock funds, a fund manager can make costly mistakes, such as not being invested when the market goes up, being too aggressive when the market plummets, or just being in the wrong stocks. An actively managed fund can easily underperform the overall market index that it's competing against.

_____

_____

_____

In addition to having lower operating expenses, which help boost your returns, index mutual funds and ETFs based on an index are usually tax-friendlier when you invest outside retirement accounts. Fund managers of actively managed portfolios, in their attempts to increase returns, buy and sell securities more frequently. However, this trading increases a fund's taxable capital gains distributions and reduces a fund's after-tax return.

Vanguard is the largest and best fund provider of index funds and ETFs because it maintains the lowest annual operating fees in the business. Vanguard has all types of bond and stock (both US and international) index funds.

Asset Allocation

Asset allocation simply means you decide what percentage of your investments you place — or allocate — into bonds versus stocks and into international stocks versus US stocks.

When you invest money for the longer term, such as for retirement, you can choose among the various types of funds that I discuss in this chapter. Most people get a big headache when they try to decide how to spread their money among the choices. This section helps you begin cutting through the clutter.

Allocating for the long term

Many working folks have time on their side, and they need to use that time to make their money grow. You may have two or more decades before you need to draw on some portion of your retirement account assets. If some of your investments drop a bit over a year or two — or even over five years — the value of your investments has plenty of time to recover before you spend the money in retirement.

Your current age and the number of years until you retire are the biggest factors in your allocation decision. The younger you are and the more years you have before retirement, the more comfortable you should be with volatile, growth-oriented investments, such as stock funds. (See Chapter 2 for the risks and historic returns of different investments.)

Table 9-1 lists guidelines for allocating fund money that you've earmarked for long-term purposes such as retirement.

Your Investment Attitude	Bond Fund Allocation (%)	Stock Fund Allocation (%)
Conservative	= Age	= 100 – Age
Middle of the road	= Age – 10	= 110 – Age
Aggressive	= Age – 20	= 120 – Age

Table 9-1: *Asset Allocation for the Long Haul*

What's it all mean, you ask? Consider this example: If you're a conservative sort who doesn't like a lot of risk, but you recognize the value of striving for some growth to make your money work harder, you're a middle-of-the-road type. Using Table 9-1, if you're 35 years old, you may consider putting 25 percent (35 – 10) into bond funds and 75 percent (110 – 35) into stock funds.

Now divvy up your stock investment money between US and international funds. Here's what portion of your stock allocation I recommend investing in overseas stocks:

- 20 percent (for a play-it-safe attitude)
- 35 percent (for a middle-of-the-road attitude)
- 50 percent (for an aggressive attitude)

Using Table 9-1, if a 35-year-old, middle-of-the-road investor puts 75 percent in stocks, she can then invest about 35 percent of the stock fund investments (which works out to be around 25 percent of the total) in international stock funds. So here's what the 35-year-old, middle-of-the-road investor's portfolio asset allocation looks like:

Bonds	25%
US stocks	50%
International stocks	25%

Diversifying your stock fund investments

Suppose your investment allocation decisions suggest that you invest 50 percent in US stock funds. Which ones do you choose? You can choose from growth-oriented stocks and funds and those that focus on value stocks as well as from funds that focus on small-, medium-, or large-company stocks. (I explain these types of stocks and funds in Chapter 10.) You also need to decide what portion you want to invest in index funds (which I discuss earlier in "Consider index funds") versus actively managed funds that try to beat the market.

Generally, it's a good idea to diversify using different types of funds. You can diversify in one of two ways:

- **Purchase several individual funds, each of which focuses on a different style.** For example, you can invest in a large-company value stock fund and in a small-company growth fund. I find this approach somewhat tedious. Granted, it does allow a fund manager to specialize and gain greater knowledge about a particular type of stock. But many of the best managers invest in more than one narrow range of security.

- **Invest in a handful of funds (five to ten), each of which covers several bases and that together cover them all.** Remember, the investment delineations are somewhat arbitrary, and most funds focus on more than just one type of investment. For example, a fund may focus on small-company value stocks but may also invest in medium-company stocks. It may also invest in some that are more growth oriented.

Deciding how much you should use index versus actively managed funds is a matter of personal taste. If you're satisfied knowing you'll get the market rate of return and you can't underperform the market (after accounting for your costs), index your entire portfolio. On the other hand, if you enjoy the challenge of trying to pick the better managers and want the potential to earn better than the market level of returns, don't use index funds at all. Investing in a happy medium of both is always a safe bet.

10

Selecting Mutual Funds and ETFs

I'm not exaggerating when I say there are hundreds of thousands of mutual and exchange-traded funds to choose from. You can begin to sift through them and select the ones that are best for your situation by understanding the categories the funds are divided into. This chapter gives you details about those categories and how they're further broken down.

Stock Funds

The best stock mutual and exchange-traded funds are excellent investment vehicles that reduce your risk, compared to purchasing individual stocks, because they

- **Invest in dozens of stocks:** Unless you possess a lot of money to invest, you're likely to buy only a handful of stocks. If you end up with a lemon in your portfolio, it can devastate your other good choices. If such a stock represents 20 percent of your holdings, the rest of your stock selections need to increase about 25 percent in value just to get you back to even. Stock funds mitigate this risk.

  For example, if a fund holds equal amounts of 50 stocks and one goes to zero, you lose only 2 percent of the fund value if the stock was an average holding. Similarly, if the fund holds 100 stocks, you lose just 1 percent.

- **Invest in different types of stocks:** Some funds invest in stocks of different sizes of companies in a variety of industries. Others may hold US and international stocks. Different types of stocks (explained in the upcoming section "Different types of stock funds") generally don't move in tandem. So if smaller-company stocks get beat up, larger-company stocks may fare better. If US stocks are in the tank, international stocks may be on an upswing.

Making money with stock funds

When you invest in stock funds, you can make money in three ways:

- **Dividends:** As a fund investor, you can choose to receive your share of the dividends paid out to the fund as cash or to reinvest them in purchasing more shares in the fund. Higher-growth companies tend to pay lower dividends.

  Unless you need the income to live on (if, for example, you're already retired), reinvest your dividends into buying more shares in the fund. If you reinvest outside of a retirement account, keep a record of those reinvestments because you need to factor those additional purchases into the tax calculations you make when you sell your shares. (Most brokers will allow you to reinvest dividends paid on ETFs without a fee.)

- **Capital gains distributions:** When a fund manager sells stocks for more than he paid, the resulting profits, known as *capital gains*, must be netted against losses and paid out to the fund's shareholders. Just as with

dividends, you can reinvest your capital gains distributions in the fund.

- **Appreciation:** The fund manager isn't going to sell all
the stocks that have gone up in value. Thus, the price
per share of the fund increases to reflect the gains in
its stock holdings. For you, these profits are on paper
until you sell the fund and lock them in. Of course,
if a fund's stocks decline in value, the share price
depreciates.

If you add together dividends, capital gains distributions,
and appreciation, you arrive at the *total return* of a fund.

Different types of stock funds

Stock funds and the stocks they invest in are usually pigeon-
holed into particular categories based on the types of stocks
they focus on. Categorizing stock funds is often tidier in theory than in practice, though, because some funds invest in
an eclectic mix of stocks. So don't get bogged down with the
names of funds — they sometimes have misleading names and
don't necessarily do what those names imply. The investment

strategies of the fund and the fund's typical investments are what matter. The following characteristics are what you need to pay attention to:

- **Company size:** The first dimension on which a stock fund's stock selection differs is based on the size of the companies in which the fund invests — small, medium, or large. The total market value *(capitalization)* of a company's outstanding stock defines the categories that define the stocks that the fund invests in. (The term *capitalization* is often shortened to "cap," so you may hear financial folks tossing around terms like *large cap* and *small cap*.)

  - **Small-capitalization stocks** are usually defined as stocks of companies that possess total market capitalization of less than $2 billion.

  - **Medium-capitalization stocks** have market values between $2 billion and $10 billion.

  - **Large-capitalization stocks** are those of companies with market values greater than $10 billion.

- **Growth versus value:** Stock fund managers and their funds are further categorized by whether they invest in growth or value stocks:

  - **Growth stocks** have high prices in relation to the company's assets, profits, and potential profits. Growth companies typically experience rapidly expanding revenues and profits. These companies tend to reinvest most of their earnings in the company to fuel future expansion; thus, these stocks pay low dividends.

  - **Value stocks** are priced cheaply in relation to the company's assets, profits, and potential profits. Value stocks tend to pay higher dividends and historically have produced higher total returns than growth stocks.

Fund companies sometimes use other terms to describe other types of stock funds. *Aggressive growth funds* tend to invest in the most growth-oriented companies and may undertake riskier investment practices, such as frequent trading. *Growth and income funds* tend to invest

_____

_____

_____

in stocks that pay higher-than-average dividends, thus offering the investor the potential for growth and income. *Income funds* tend to invest more in higher-yielding stocks. Bonds usually make up the other portion of income funds.

- **Company location:** Stocks and the companies that issue them are also divvied up based on the location of their main operations and headquarters. Funds that specialize in US stocks are called *US stock funds;* those focusing in overseas stocks are typically called *international* or *overseas funds.*

Putting together two or three of these major classifications, you can start to comprehend all of those lengthy names that fund companies give their stock funds. You can have funds that focus on large-company value stocks or small-company growth stocks. You can add in US, international, and worldwide funds to further subdivide these categories into more fund types. So you can have international stock funds that focus on small-company stocks or growth stocks.

You can purchase several stock funds, each focusing on a different type of stock, to diversify into various types of stocks. Two potential advantages result from doing so:

- Not all your money rides in one stock fund and with one fund manager.
- Each of the different fund managers looks at and tracks particular stock investment possibilities.

The following sections describe the best stock funds that are worthy of your consideration. The funds differ primarily in terms of the types of stocks that they invest in. Keep in mind as you read through these funds that they also differ in their tax friendliness (see Chapter 3). However, if you invest inside a retirement account, you don't need to worry about tax friendliness.

US stock funds

Of all the different types of funds offered, US stock funds are the largest category. Stock funds differ mainly in the size of the companies they invest in and whether the funds focus on growth or value companies. Some funds hold all these characteristics, and some funds may even invest a bit overseas.

The only way to know for sure where a fund currently invests is to ask. You can call the fund company that you're interested in to start your information search, or you can visit the company's website. You can also read the fund's annual report. Don't waste your time looking for this information in the fund's prospectus because it doesn't give you anything beyond general parameters that guide the range of investments. The prospectus generally doesn't tell you what the fund currently invests in or has invested in.

For funds you hold outside of retirement accounts, you owe current income tax on distributed dividends and capital gains. As I discuss in Chapter 3, long-term capital gains and stock dividends are taxed at lower rates than ordinary income and other investment income.

International stock funds

For diversification and growth potential, you should include in your portfolio stock funds that invest overseas. Normally, you can tell that you're looking at a fund that focuses its investments overseas if its name contains words such as *international* (foreign only), *global* (foreign and US), or *worldwide* (foreign and US).

As a general rule, avoid foreign funds that invest in just one country, regardless of whether that country is Australia, Zimbabwe, or one in between. As with investing in a sector fund that specializes in a particular industry (see the following section), this lack of diversification defeats the purpose of investing in funds. Funds that focus on specific regions, such as Southeast Asia, are better but still generally problematic because of poor diversification and higher expenses than other, more-diversified international funds.

If you want to invest in more geographically limiting international funds, take a look at T. Rowe Price's and Vanguard's offerings, which invest in broader regions, such as just Europe, Asia, and the volatile but higher-growth-potential emerging markets in Southeast Asia and Latin America.

In addition to the risks normally inherent with stock fund investing, changes in the value of foreign currencies relative to the US dollar cause price changes in the international securities. A decline in the value of the US dollar helps the value of foreign stock funds (and conversely, a rising dollar versus other currencies can reduce the value of foreign stocks). Some foreign stock funds hedge against currency changes.

Although this hedging helps reduce volatility a bit, it does cost money.

Sector funds

Sector funds invest in securities in specific industries. In most cases, you should avoid sector funds for several reasons, including the following:

- **Lack of diversification:** Investing in stocks of a single industry defeats a major purpose of investing in funds — you give up the benefits of diversification. Also, even if you're lucky enough to jump into a sector fund just before it becomes "hot," you can't assume that the fund will pick the right securities within that sector.

- **High fees:** They tend to carry much higher fees than other funds.

- **Taxable distributions:** Many sector funds have high rates of trading or turnover of their investment holdings. Investors who use these funds outside of retirement accounts have to pay the tax man for the likely greater taxable distributions that this trading produces.

Bond Funds

Bond funds can make you money in the same three ways that a stock fund can: dividends, capital gains distributions, and appreciation. (See the earlier section "Making money with stock funds" for more on these ways of making money.) However, most of the time, the bulk of your return in a bond fund comes from dividends.

Although an overwhelming number of bond fund choices exists, not that many remain after you eliminate high-cost funds (those with loads and high ongoing fees), low-performance funds (which are often the high-cost funds), and funds managed by fund companies and fund managers with minimal experience investing in bonds. Here are the aspects to consider when choosing bond funds:

- **Length to maturity:** Bond fund objectives and names usually fit one of three maturity categories — short-, intermediate-, and long-term. You can earn a higher yield from investing in a bond fund that holds longer-term bonds, but such bond prices are more sensitive to changes in interest rates.

- **Quality:** Generally speaking, the lower their issuer's credit rating, the riskier the bond. As with the risk associated with longer maturities, a fund that holds lower-quality bonds should provide higher returns for the increased risk you take. A higher yield is the bond market's way of compensating you for taking greater risk. Funds holding higher-quality bonds provide lower returns but more security.

- **Loads and fees:** After you settle on the type of bonds you want, you must consider a bond fund's costs, including its sales commissions and annual operating fees. Stick with no-load funds that maintain lower annual operating expenses.

- **Tax implications:** Pay attention to the taxability of the dividends that bonds pay. If you're investing in bonds inside of retirement accounts, you want taxable bonds. If you invest in bonds outside of retirement accounts, the choice between taxable versus tax-free depends on your tax bracket (see Chapter 3).

Bond funds fluctuate in value, so invest in them only if you have sufficient money in an emergency reserve.

Yield-related missteps

When selecting bond funds to invest in, investors are often led astray as to how much they can expect to make. The first mistake is to look at recent performance and assume you'll get that return in the future. Investing in bond funds based on recent performance is particularly tempting immediately after a period where interest rates have declined because declines in interest rates pump up bond prices and therefore bond fund total returns. Remember that an equal but opposite force waits to counteract pumped-up bond returns: Bond prices fall when interest rates rise.

Don't get me wrong: Past performance is an important issue to consider. In order for performance numbers to be meaningful and useful, you must compare bond funds that are comparable.

Bond funds calculate their yield after subtracting their operating expenses. When you contact a fund company seeking a fund's current yield, make sure you understand what time period the yield covers. Fund companies are supposed to give you the SEC yield, which is a standard yield calculation that allows for fairer comparisons among bond funds. The SEC yield, which reflects the bond fund's yield to maturity, is the best yield to use when you compare funds because it captures the effective rate of interest that an investor can receive in the future.

Unfortunately, if you select bond funds based on advertised yield, you're quite likely to purchase the wrong bond funds. Bond funds and the fund companies that sell them can play more than a few games to fatten a fund's yield. But yield-enhancing shenanigans can leave you poorer. Here's what you need to watch out for:

- **Lower quality:** When comparing one short-term bond fund to another, you may discover that one pays 0.5 percentage points more and decide it looks better. However, you may find out later that the higher-yielding fund invests 20 percent of its money in junk (non-investment grade) bonds, whereas the other fund fully invests in high-quality bonds.

- **Longer maturities:** Bond funds can usually increase their yield just by increasing their maturity a bit. So if one long-term bond fund invests in bonds that mature in an average of 17 years and another fund has an average maturity of 12 years, comparing the two is a classic case of comparing apples and oranges.

- **Giving your money back without your knowing it:** Some funds return a portion of your principal in the form of dividends. This move artificially pumps up a fund's yield but depresses its total return. When you compare bond funds, make sure you compare their total return over time (in addition to making sure the funds have comparable portfolios of bonds).

- **Waiving of expenses:** Some bond funds, particularly newer ones, waive a portion or even all of their operating expenses to temporarily inflate the fund's yield. Bond funds that engage in this practice often end sales quietly when the bond market is performing well. Don't forget that if you sell a bond fund (held outside of a retirement account) that has appreciated in value, you owe taxes on your profits.

Actively managed bond funds

Some bond funds are aggressively managed. Managers of these funds possess a fair degree of latitude to purchase and trade bonds that they think will perform best in the future. For example, if a fund manager thinks interest rates will rise, she usually buys shorter-term bonds and keeps more of a fund's assets in cash. The fund manager may invest more in lower-credit-quality bonds if she thinks the economy is improving and that more companies will prosper and improve their credit standing.

Aggressively managed funds are a gamble. If interest rates fall instead of rise, the fund manager who moved into shorter-term bonds and cash experiences worse performance. If interest rates fall because the economy sinks into recession, the lower-credit-quality bonds will likely suffer from a higher default rate and depress the fund's performance even further.

It's fine to invest some of your bond fund money in funds that try to hold the best position for changes in the economy and interest rates, but remember that if these fund managers are wrong, you can lose more money. Over the long term, you'll probably do best with efficiently managed funds that stick with an investment objective and that don't try to time and predict the bond market. Index funds (and their companion exchange-traded funds) that invest in a relatively fixed basket of bonds so as to track a market index of bond prices are a good example of this passive approach.

Short-term bond funds

Of all bond funds, short-term bond funds are the least sensitive to interest rate fluctuations. The stability of short-term bond funds makes them appropriate investments for money that you seek a better rate of return on than a money market fund can produce. But with short-term bond funds, you also have to tolerate the risk of losing a percent or two in principal value if interest rates rise.

 Short-term bonds work well for money you earmark for use in a few years, such as the purchase of a home or a car, or for money you plan to withdraw from your retirement account in the near future.

Intermediate-term bond funds

Intermediate-term bond funds hold bonds that typically mature in a decade or so. They're more volatile than shorter-term bonds but can also prove more rewarding. The longer you own an intermediate-term bond fund, the more likely you are to earn a higher return on it than on a short-term fund, unless interest rates continue to rise over many years.

_____

_____

_____

As an absolute minimum, don't purchase an intermediate-term fund unless you expect to hold it for three to five years — or even longer, if you can. You need to make sure the money you put into an intermediate-term fund is money you don't expect to use in the near future.

Long-term bond funds

Long-term bond funds are the most aggressive and volatile bond funds around. If interest rates on long-term bonds increase substantially, you can easily see the principal value of your investment decline 10 percent or more. (See Chapter 8 for a discussion of how interest rate changes impact bond prices.)

 Long-term bond funds are generally used for retirement investing in one of two situations:

• Investors don't expect to tap their investment money for a decade or more.

• Investors want to maximize current dividend income and are willing to tolerate volatility.

_____

_____

_____

Don't use these funds to invest money that you plan to use within the next five years, because a bond market drop can leave your portfolio short of your monetary goal.

Subcategories of bond funds

Short-, intermediate-, and long-term bond funds can be divided into subcategories based on their tax advantages. Here's the breakdown:

- **Taxable bond funds:** Consider bond funds that pay taxable dividends when you're not in a high tax bracket and for investing inside of retirement accounts. However, be careful of taxable long-term bond funds; they're generally much more volatile than most bond funds.

- **US Treasury bond funds:** US Treasury bond funds may be appropriate if you prefer a bond fund that invests in US Treasuries (which possess the safety of government backing; see Chapter 8 for details). They're also a fine choice if you're not in a high federal tax bracket but you're in a high state tax bracket (5 percent or higher). I don't recommend Treasuries for retirement accounts because they pay less interest than fully taxable bond funds.

- **Federally tax-free bond funds:** If you're in a high federal bracket but in a low state bracket (less than 5 percent), consider investing in federally tax-free bond funds (whose dividends are state taxable).

- **State and federally tax-free long-term bond funds:** State and federally tax-free bond funds are scarce. State and federally tax-free *long-term* bond funds may be appropriate when you're in high federal *and* high state (5 percent or higher) tax brackets.

Balanced and Asset Allocation Funds

Hybrid funds invest in a mixture of different types of securities. Most commonly, they invest in both bonds and stocks. These funds are usually less risky and less volatile than funds that invest exclusively in stocks; in an economic downturn, bonds usually hold value better than stocks.

Hybrid funds make it easier for investors who are skittish about investing in stocks to hold stocks because the hybrids reduce the volatility that normally comes with pure stock funds. Because of their extensive diversification, hybrid funds are excellent choices for an investor who doesn't have much money to start with.

Hybrid funds come in two forms:

- **Balanced funds** generally try to maintain a fairly constant percentage of investment in stocks and bonds.

- **Asset allocation funds,** by contrast, normally adjust the mix of different investments according to the portfolio manager's expectations.

Some asset allocation funds, however, tend to keep more of a fixed mix of stocks and bonds, whereas some balanced funds shift the mix around quite frequently. (Although the concept of a manager being in the right place at the right time and beating the market averages sounds good in theory, most funds that shift assets fail to outperform a buy-and-hold approach.)

Because hybrid funds pay decent dividends from the bonds they hold, they're not appropriate for some investors who purchase funds outside tax-sheltered retirement accounts. Avoid hybrid funds if you're in a higher tax bracket. (Chapter 7 has details on tax-free bonds.) You should consider buying separate tax-friendly stock funds and tax-free bond funds (both discussed earlier in this chapter) to create your own hybrid portfolio.

Money Market Funds

As I explain in Chapter 7, money market funds are a safe, higher-yielding alternative to bank accounts. (If you're in a higher tax bracket, money market funds have even more appeal because you can get tax-free versions of money market funds.) Under Securities and Exchange Commission regulations, money market funds can invest only in the highest-credit-rated securities, and their investments must have an average maturity of less than 60 days. The short-term nature of these securities effectively eliminates the risk of money market funds being sensitive to changes in interest rates.

The securities that money market funds use are extremely safe. General-purpose money market funds invest in government-backed securities, bank certificates of deposit, and short-term corporate debt that the largest and most creditworthy companies and the US government issue.

When shopping for a money market fund, consider these factors:

- **Expenses:** Within a given category of money market funds (general, Treasury, municipal, and so on), fund managers invest in the same basic securities. The market for these securities is pretty darn efficient, so "superstar" money market fund managers may eke out an extra 0.1 percent per year in yield but not much more.

   Select a money market fund that does a good job controlling its expenses. The operating expenses that the fund deducts before payment of dividends are the biggest determinant of yield. All other things being equal (which they usually are with different money market funds), lower operating expenses translate into higher yields for you.

You have no need or reason to tolerate annual operating expenses of greater than 0.5 percent. Some top-quality funds charge 0.3 percent or less annually. Remember, lower expenses don't mean a fund company cuts corners or provides poor service. Lower expenses are possible in most cases because a fund company is successful in attracting a lot of money to invest.

- **Tax consequences:** With money market funds, all your return comes from dividends. What you actually get to keep of these returns (on non-retirement account investments) is what's left after the federal and state governments take their cut of your investment income. If you invest money that's held outside of a retirement account and you're in a high tax bracket, you may come out ahead if you invest in tax-free money market funds. If you're in a high-tax state, then a state money market fund, if good ones exist for your state, may be a sound move.

  Tax-free refers to the taxability of the dividends that the fund pays. You don't get a tax deduction for money that you put into the fund, as you do with 401(k) or other retirement-type accounts.

- **Location of other funds:** Consider what other investing you plan to do at the fund company where you establish a money market fund. Suppose you decide to make fund investments in stocks and bonds at T. Rowe Price. In that case, keeping a money market fund at a different firm that offers a slightly higher yield may not be worth the time and administrative hassle, especially if you don't plan on holding much cash in your money market fund.

- **Associated services:** Good money market funds offer other useful services, such as free check writing, telephone exchange and redemptions, and automated electronic exchange services with your bank account.

Taxable money market funds

Money market funds that pay taxable dividends may be appropriate for retirement account funds that await investment as well as for non-retirement account money when you're not in a high federal tax bracket *and* aren't in a high state tax bracket (less than 5 percent).

US Treasury money market funds

Consider US Treasury money market funds if you prefer a money market fund that invests in US Treasuries, which maintain the safety of government backing, or if you're not in a high federal tax bracket but *are* in a high state tax bracket (5 percent or higher).

Municipal money market funds

Municipal (also known as *muni*) money market funds invest in short-term debt that state and local governments issue. A municipal money market fund, which pays you federally tax-free dividends, invests in munis issued by state and local governments throughout the country. A state-specific municipal fund invests in state and local government-issued munis for one state, such as New York. So if you live in New York and buy a New York municipal fund, the dividends on that fund are federal and New York state-tax-free.

So how do you decide whether to buy a nationwide or state-specific municipal money market fund? Money market funds that are only federally tax-free may be appropriate when you're in a high federal tax bracket but not in a high state bracket (less than 5 percent). State-tax-free municipal money market funds are worth considering when you're in a high federal *and* a high state tax bracket (5 percent or higher).

11

Brokerage Firms

When you invest in certain securities — such as stocks and bonds and exchange-traded funds — and when you also wish to hold mutual funds from different companies in a single account, you need brokerage services. Brokers execute your trades to buy or sell stocks, bonds, and other securities and enable you to centralize your holdings of mutual funds and other investments.

In this chapter, I explain the ins and outs of discount brokers and online brokers to help you find the right one for your investment needs.

Discount Brokers

Discount brokers charge lower fees, known as *commissions*, than many traditional brokerage firms do to trade stocks and bonds. Discount brokers, which include many online brokers, abound and continue to capture the lion's share of new business. Many do stock trades, regardless of size, for a flat rate of less than $40, and some do them for less than $20 or even $10 per transaction.

When you hear the word *discount*, you probably think of adjectives like *cheap, inferior quality,* and such. However, in the securities brokerage field, the discount brokers who place your trades at substantial discounts can offer you even better value and service than high-cost brokers. The following list offers some of the reasons discount brokers give you more bang for your buck:

- They can place your trades at a substantially lower price because they have much lower overhead.

- They tend not to rent posh downtown office space that comes with a premium rent.

- They don't waste tons of money employing economists and research analysts to produce forecasts and predictive reports.

In addition to lower commissions, another major benefit of using discount brokers is that they generally work on salary. Working on salary removes a significant conflict of interest that continues to get commission-paid brokers and their firms into trouble. People who sell on commission to make a living aren't bad people, but given the financial incentives they have, don't expect to receive holistic, in-your-best-interest investing counsel from them.

The truth about discount brokers

One of the many sales tactics of high-commission brokerage firms is to try to disparage discounters by telling you, "You'll receive poor service from discounters." My own experience, as well as that of others, suggests that in many cases, discounters actually offer *better* service.

Many of the larger discounters with convenient branch offices offer assistance with filling out paperwork and access to independent research reports. From discounters, you also can buy *no-load* (commission-free) mutual funds that are run by management teams that make investment decisions for you. Such funds can be bought from mutual fund companies as well. (See Chapters 9 and 10 for more on these mutual funds.)

High-commission firms used to argue that discount brokerage customers received worse trade prices when they bought and sold. This assertion is a bogus argument because all brokerage firms use a computer-based trading system for smaller retail trades. Trades are processed in seconds. High-commission brokers also say that discounters are only "for people who know exactly what they're doing and don't need any help." This statement is also false, especially given the abundance of financial information and advice available today.

Selecting a discount broker

Which discount broker is best for you depends on what your needs and wants are. In addition to fees, consider how important having a local branch office is to you. If you seek to invest in mutual funds, the discount brokerage firms I list later in this section offer access to good funds (you can access all exchange-traded funds through a broker because ETFs trade like stocks on exchanges). In addition, these firms offer money market funds into which you can deposit money awaiting investment or proceeds from a sale.

Within the discount brokerage business, *deep discounters* are firms that offer the lowest rates but fewer frills and other services. Generally, deep discounters don't have local branch offices like big discounters do, and they also don't offer money market funds with the highest yields.

Be careful of some deep discounters that offer bargain commissions but earn money on your account in other ways, such as by charging high fees for particular services or offering below-market interest rates on money awaiting investment.

Here are my top picks for discount brokers:

- **T. Rowe Price (800-225-5132;** `www.troweprice.com`**):** T. Rowe Price offers a solid family of no-load mutual funds. The company's brokerage fees are competitive and among those on the lower end for discounters.

- **Vanguard (800-992-8327;** `www.vanguard.com`**):** Vanguard is best known for its excellent family of no-load mutual funds, but its discount brokerage services have improved over the years. Vanguard has also reduced its brokerage fees in recent years, and its prices are now near the low end of discount brokers.

- **TD Ameritrade (800-454-9272;** www.tdameritrade.
  com**):** TD Ameritrade offers competitive commission
  rates and more than 100 branch offices.

All the preceding firms offer mutual funds from many fund
companies in addition to their family of funds (if they have a
family of funds). In other words, you may purchase mutual
funds that aren't in the T. Rowe Price family of funds through
the T. Rowe Price brokerage department. Other discounters
have good service and competitive rates, so shop around if you
desire. Note, however, that you generally pay a transaction fee
to buy funds from firms that don't offer their own family of
funds.

Absent from my list are the large discounters Fidelity and
Charles Schwab. The simple reason they're missing is that they
charge significantly higher transaction fees than the competition does. These firms can get away with premium pricing,
despite comparable services, because enough investors prefer to do business with name-brand companies. Although I
think that both companies can offer investors a fine base from
which to do their investing, I don't feel that their fees are justi-
fied unless you want to do business with a broker that maintains a branch office in your area. If you're going to invest in

individual stocks (as discussed in Chapter 6), Charles Schwab and Fidelity deserve more consideration because they offer a comprehensive array of useful and independent research resources.

Online Brokers

To get the lowest trading commissions, you generally must place your trades online. Visit any website that's remotely related to investing in stocks, and you're sure to find ads for various Internet brokers. Anyone familiar with the economics of running a brokerage firm can tell you that technology, when properly applied, reduces a broker's labor costs. Some brokerages — thanks to technology — can now perform *market orders* (which means they'll execute your trade at the best current available price) for a few bucks. Hence the attraction of online trading.

Before you jump at the chance to save a few dollars by trading online, read the following sections for other considerations that should factor in to your choice of an online broker — or your decision to trade online at all.

Online trading motives

If trading online attracts you, first examine why. If you're motivated by how easily you can check account balances, beware. Tracking prices daily (or, worse, minute by minute) and frequently checking your account balances leads to addictive trading. A low fee of $5 or $10 per trade doesn't really save you any money if you trade a lot and rack up significant total commissions, and you pay more in capital gains taxes when you sell at a profit. Don't forget that as with trading through a regular brokerage firm, you also lose the *spread* (difference between the bid and ask prices when you trade stocks and bonds) and incur the explicit commission rates that online brokers charge.

Frankly, trading online is also an unfortunately easy way for people to act impulsively and emotionally when making important investment decisions. If you're prone to such actions or if you find yourself tracking and trading investments too closely, stay away from this form of trading and use the Internet only to check account information and gather factual information.

Most of the best investment firms also allow you to trade via phone. In most cases, phone trading is discounted when you compare it to trading through a live broker, although it's admittedly less glamorous than trading through a website.

Some brokers also offer account information and trading capabilities via apps and smartphones, which may add to your costs. Trading through such handheld technology can also promote addictive investment behaviors.

Other costs

Online brokerage customers often shop for low costs. However, shopping merely for low-cost trading prices often causes investors to overlook other important issues. The biggest problem is firms that nickel-and-dime you with fees. For instance, some charge fees for real-time stock quotes (as opposed to quotes that may be 15 to 20 minutes old and are free). Other brokers charge $20 here and $50 there for services such as wiring money or simply closing your account. Also beware of "inactivity fees" that some brokers levy on accounts that have infrequent trading. So before you sign up with any broker, make sure you examine its entire fee schedule.

Also beware below-market rates on money market accounts with many cut-rate brokers. When you buy or sell an investment, you may have cash sitting around in your brokerage account. Not surprisingly, the online brokers pitching their cheap online trading rates in 3-inch-high numbers don't reveal their money market rates in such large type (if at all). Some don't pay interest on the first $1,000 or so of your cash balance, and even then, some companies pay half a percent to a full percent less than their best competitors.

Service quality

Common complaints among customers of online brokers include slow responses to email queries, long wait times to speak with a person to answer questions or resolve problems, delays in opening accounts and receiving literature, unclear statements, incorrect processing of trading requests, and slow web response during periods of heavy traffic.

When you shop for an online broker, check your prospects thoroughly. Here are some things to do:

- **Call for literature and to see how long it takes you to reach a live human being.** Ask some questions and see how knowledgeable and helpful the representatives are. For non-retirement accounts, if you want to gauge the quality of the firm's year-end account statements, ask prospective brokerages to send you a sample. If you're a mutual fund investor, check out the quality of the funds that the company offers. In other words, don't allow the sheer number of funds that the company offers impress you. Also, inquire about the interest rates that the company pays on cash balances. Try sending some questions to the broker's website and see how accurate and timely the response is.

- **Consider checking online forums to see what current and past customers say about the firms you're considering.** Most online brokers that have been around for more than six months lay claim to a number-one rating with some survey or ranking of online brokers. Place little value on such claims.

- **Examine what the firm did before it got into the online brokerage business.** Would you rather put your money and trust in the hands of an established and respected financial service company that has been around for a number of years or an upstart firm run by a couple of people hoping to strike it rich on the Internet? Transact business only with firms that offer sufficient account insurance (enough to protect your assets) through the Securities Investor Protection

Corporation (SIPC). The severe stock market downturns in the early and late 2000s led to major shakeouts, and you need to protect yourself.

The best online brokers

Among the e-brokers I've reviewed, my top picks are the following:

Broker	Phone Number	Website
E*Trade	800-387-2331	etrade.com
Scottrade	800-619-7283	scottrade.com
T. Rowe Price	800-638-5660	troweprice.com
Vanguard	800-992-8327	vanguard.com
TD Ameritrade	800-934-4448	tdameritrade.com

12

Internet Resources

Because people interested in managing their money surf the Internet today more than ever, thousands of websites have sprung up to meet the demand. Although the low barriers to entry in the online world make it easy for scammers to flog their wares and flawed advice, this medium can offer some helpful resources if you know where to look and how to discern the good from the not-so-good.

Although you may be smart enough to avoid offers that promise pie in the sky, you're far more likely to fall for unsound financial advice, which is abundant online. You can find plenty of self-serving advertorial content and bad advice online, so you should be wary and cautious. This chapter offers tips for evaluating Internet resources.

Assessing Online Resources

Fraud and bad financial advice existed long before the Internet came around. The Securities and Exchange Commission (SEC) describes online scams as "new medium, same message." But don't worry. The tips in the following sections can help you find the nuggets of helpful online advice and avoid the land mines.

Being aware of agendas

Get an idea of who's behind a site before you trust its information. Some sites go to extraordinary lengths — including providing lots of information and advice and attempting to conceal the identity of the company that runs the site — to disguise their agendas. Therefore, don't turn to the web for advice or opinions because the advice and opinions you find usually aren't objective. Similarly, approach online financial calculators with skepticism; most are simplistic and biased.

Many websites and blogs have icons (or About tabs) that you can click on to see some background regarding the site's sponsor and to find out whether the site solicits potential advertisers. One click can show you that a site purporting to be a reference service of the best small-company stocks to invest in may be nothing more than an online Yellow Pages of companies that paid the site an advertising fee. Look for sites that exercise quality control in what they post and that use sensible screening criteria for outside information or companies they list.

Just because every Tom, Dick, and Jane can easily and at a relatively low cost set up an Internet site or blog doesn't mean that their sites and advice are worthy of your time. Not surprisingly, the financial companies with reputations for integrity offline are the ones that offer some of the best integrity online. For example, the leading and most investor-friendly investment companies often have the best education-oriented websites.

Soliciting grassroots customer feedback

The Internet can be a useful place to do consumer research. The more enlightening online conversations that I encounter usually start with someone asking what others thought about particular financial service firms, such as brokerage firms. If you're investigating a certain financial service, the Internet can be an efficient way to get feedback from other people who have worked with that firm.

_____

_____

_____

Go online to find people who have done business with a given firm. You can read customer review sites such as www.planetfeedback.com, www.yelp.com, or Google reviews. As in the offline world, though, don't believe everything you hear.

Fact checking to verify online information

Enhance the value of the online information you gather by verifying it elsewhere. You can do some fact checking both online and offline. For example, if you're contemplating the purchase of some stock based on financial data that you read on an investing site, first check out those numbers at the library or at one of the websites I recommend later in this chapter.

Lots of Internet investment advice (and most of the scams) focuses on smaller companies and investment start-ups; unfortunately, these are often the most difficult businesses to locate information about. The SEC requires companies that are raising less than $1 million to file a Form D, so you should check to see whether a small company that's soliciting you has filed one.

To inquire whether a company has filed Form D, call the SEC's Office of Investor Education and Advocacy at 800-732-0330 or send an email to publicinfo@sec.gov. Also check with your state securities regulator. For contact information for state regulators, call the North American Securities Administrators Association at 202-737-0900 or visit its website at www.nasaa.org.

If something sounds too good to be true, check out and possibly report your concerns to Internet fraud-fighting organization sites. In addition to the SEC's website, check out the Financial Industry Regulatory Authority website (www.finra.org) and the National Consumers League's Fraud Information Center (www.fraud.org; 202-835-3323).

Picking the Best Investment Websites

The quality of the investing information that's on the Internet is gradually improving, and a handful of sites are setting a high standard. In the following sections, I provide my top picks for those investing sites that are worthy of your online time.

CorporateInformation.com

CorporateInformation.com (http://corporate information.com) is owned and operated by Wright Investors' Services, which, in addition to managing money for affluent individuals, publishes comprehensive reports on thousands of companies around the globe. Those who are interested in web-based stock research will also enjoy the many links to other Internet-investing and research sites. This site also provides plenty of current business news.

Morningstar.com

The behemoth of the mutual fund data business, Morningstar. com, has a website (www.morningstar.com) that provides information and tools for mutual fund and stock research. The basic stuff is free, but you have to pay $199 per year to access the analyst reports, stock research reports, and other premium content. In addition to providing more data than you could ever possibly digest on funds and stocks, this site also includes short, insightful articles that are useful to more educated investors.

Sec.gov

All publicly held companies and mutual funds must file annual and quarterly reports and other documents electronically with the US Securities and Exchange Commission. This information is easily accessible for free (paid for by tax dollars) on the SEC website (`www.sec.gov`).

If you're researching individual companies, you can find corporate reports — annual reports, 10-Ks, and the like — through this website. Or you can call the individual companies that interest you and ask them to mail you the desired material.

Vanguard.com

Few sites run by investment companies are worth visiting unless you're an account holder at the firm and you want to review your accounts or conduct transactions online. Here's why: Much of the content is self-serving, biased, and advertorial in nature. However, the fund behemoth the Vanguard

Group operates a site (www.vanguard.com) that is the exception.

Of course, at its website, you can find details on Vanguard's fine family of funds, but you also find some useful educational materials.

If you're one of the millions of Vanguard shareholders, you can access your accounts and perform most transactions online. Vanguard's discount brokerage division, also accessible online, allows you to invest in many other fund companies' funds (as well as Vanguard's) through a single account. The company's website also enables you to link accounts that you may hold through most other financial institutions.

_____

_____

_____

About the Author

Eric Tyson, MBA, is a best-selling author and syndicated columnist. Through his work, he teaches people to manage their money better and to successfully direct their own investments. Eric was a management consultant to Fortune 500 financial service firms before he started and managed his own business. He has counseled thousands of clients on a variety of investment quandaries and questions.